LIVING MAGICAL ARTS

The living magical arts
described in this book derive from
perennial philosophy and enduring
spiritual traditions; they grow from
myth, legend, visionary cosmology and
poetic insight. They do not derive
from cultism, secret elitist
movements, or any form
of anti-religion.

LIVING MAGICAL ARTS

IMAGINATION AND MAGIC FOR THE 21st CENTURY

R.J. STEWART

BLANDFORD

First published in the UK 1991 by Blandford
An imprint of Cassell plc, Villiers House
41/47 Strand, London WC2N 5JE

Originally published in hardback 1987

Reprinted 1987

Distributed in the United States by
Sterling Publishing Co, Inc,
387 Park Avenue South, New York, NY 10016-8810

Distributed in Australia by
Capricorn Link (Australia) Pty Ltd
PO Box 665, Lane Cove, NSW 2066

British Library Cataloguing in Publication Data

Stewart, R. J. (Robert J.) *1949-*
 Living magical arts: imagination and magic for the 21st
century.
 1. Magic
 I. Title
 133.43

ISBN 0-7137-2288-0

Typeset by Best-set Typesetter Ltd., Hong Kong
Printed in Great Britain by Mackays Chatham

CONTENTS

ACKNOWLEDGEMENTS

A full list of thanks for work concerning magical or wisdom traditions would be impossible to print, especially as the most significant influences are found in anonymous tales, songs, images and dreams.

Of specific importance to the development of this book are the following authors, friends and contacts: W.G. Gray; Dion Fortune; Ronald Heaver; Gareth Knight; John and Caitlin Matthews.

A number of the line drawings have been assembled from my crude scribbles by the immensely patient Felicity Bowers. None of the persons mentioned are in any way responsible for specific aspects of the text, theories or exercises.

R.J. STEWART 1987

FOREWORD

I have followed musician and composer Bob Stewart's writing with considerable interest over the past ten years. Commencing with some fascinating insights into pagan imagery in English folksong (*Where is Saint George?*, 1977), and a reconstruction of the ancient mysteries of Bath, or Aquae Sulis (*The Waters of the Gap*, 1981), he consolidated this early work with an important and seminal work on the dynamics of psychic transformation with *The Underworld Initiation* in 1985. Since then he has illustrated this theme with two books on the prophecies and life of Merlin, the archetypal magus of the British Isles (*The Prophetic Vision of Merlin* and *The Mystic Life of Merlin*).

As a trained magician in an Hermetic fraternity I have found myself approaching the dynamics of modern magic in a different direction from Bob Stewart, whose roots are in native traditions. It has been all the more rewarding and instructive therefore to find that we have come to occupy a considerable area of common ground.

Bob Stewart's approach is also refreshing because it is based firmly upon experience – as all valid magic must be.

There is no nonsense about this approach. Atavistic techniques of hypnosis, regression, entrancement and emotionalism are eschewed as out of place and time, and both fortune-telling and psychological reductionism revealed as, each in their way, misleading materialistic trivia. High magic is presented for what it is – the tuning of consciousness to other worlds or dimensions by the skilled application of magical patterns and key symbols in a process of personal transformation which can lead to profound and far-reaching practical results.

Most former textbooks on magic that aspired beyond the trivial have been based more on intellectual juggling with theoretical correspondences and alleged authorities than the fruits of actual experience. This is now changing, and with Bob Stewart I welcome the fact that 'the future of magical arts is now in the hands of actual practising magicians; such persons will create fresh imaginative traditions and methods of transforming consciousness and energy.' Bob Stewart's *Living Magical Arts* is one step on the way to providing that lively future.

Gareth Knight 1987

LIST OF ILLUSTRATIONS

PREFACE AND READER'S GUIDE

Much of this book is drawn from direct experience of the magical arts in modern life. I have found that the enduring traditions concerning awareness have been valuable in my own work as an author and composer or musician, but most of all they have enabled me to keep a constantly open mind, and have led to some astonishing and deeply rewarding experiences which I could not have encountered otherwise.

As magical arts are intimately concerned with traditions of education, rather than formal courses and textbooks, a proportion of the theory and some of the statements proposed are *traditional* rather than personal. I have made no attempt to burden the reader with continual notes as to which elements of the text are derived from my reception of magical traditions and which are from practical experience – or which, as is also the case with many aspects of this book, are drawn from more academic historical cultural research into the literature, symbolism and beliefs of our ancestors.

I would like to emphasise that magic is a set of methods arranging awareness according to patterns; it is not a truth or a religion. Nor is it even a philosophy, in the strict sense of the word, despite the echoes of profound philosophy found within magical traditions. The serious application of magical methods leads to transformation; it is the transformation that is of value, and not the methods themselves.

Much of any book on magical arts is, unfortunately but inevitably, taken up with comparisons between genuine traditions and popular misconceptions. Once these initial areas have been defined, the method of arranging awareness according to patterns can be attempted by the reader. The basis of magic is utterly practical and experiential; reams of theory and speculation may be disposed of through actual practice.

The proposition that consciousness may be transformed through

1

willed arranged patterns is sometimes found on the edges of psychology, but is usually discarded, as no hard boundaries can be found for such maps of the psyche. In magic the quibbling over maps and boundaries is ignored, for after the symbols have been applied and transformations of the individual have occurred, the validity or accuracy of the maps themselves becomes irrelevant. In other words magic does not work because its propositions are essentially real or true; it works because we become imaginatively involved in these propositions; for controlled periods of time under non-habitual circumstances, we behave as if they were true. The result of this is not, as popular fantasy about conditioning would have, that we become habituated to falsehood thus making it true for ourselves. In magical art, the magician grows through the patterns, be they true or not, and emerges beyond them into a clarity of awareness that was not possible before the experience of transition and transformation.

The controlled periods and non-habitual circumstances referred to above are, of course, the practices of meditation and ritual which are central to magical arts. These are not weird aberrations of behaviour, but specifically selected and amplified versions of common consciousness and life activity. Where magic differs from materialist psychology is that it firmly states that such activities may be carried out on levels of awareness that are not generally entered in normal living; magic then goes one step further and states that such levels are the true state or world of consciousness, and that our normal habitual state is one of deprivation.

We experience the devolved converse of this law of consciousness daily; millions of people are obliged to endure activities which they know are fruitless or even dangerous to others and unethical, yet by investing their employment with false systems of value and habit, they enable a degree of continuity, of fantasy-sharing, that holds the illusion together collectively and individually.

In magical arts, this same potential for fooling ourselves is applied in a totally different direction, to motivate inner transformation rather than outer coagulation. When the awareness of values changes (which is not the same as a change of values) the outer world may be transformed by magical means.

The methods described in the following pages are a distillation of traditions found within western culture; many of them are shared with other cultures worldwide, as human awareness is a planetary occurrence, even though its manifestations are printed through racial responses to geographical areas, to the environment and culture. Once again I would stress that magical arts restrict themselves to specific cultural symbols and traditions, not because these are intrinsically more valuable than any other set of such symbols, but because this is a method known to work. If it is more effective and powerful to apply a western tradition to the western psyche, the magician or would-be magician should do exactly that; when he or she has outgrown the tradition its cultural origin will be irrelevant, but before this magical psychic change the cultural stream of symbols is absolutely crucial and immensely valuable.

Beyond the methods outlined here, there are further methods which are the processes of the transformed consciousness; the purpose of magical arts is to enable the changes within the individual by which he or she may apprehend these further methods inwardly. This is the great adventure or Great Work spoken of in early mystical magical or alchemical writings; when we undertake this work all speculation, theorising or dispute is set aside; only total experience can meet the inner requirement for permanent changes of awareness.

HOW TO USE THIS BOOK

The theory and practice developed in the following chapters is founded upon a number of key concepts. Although these are discussed in detail in the main text, a summary may be helpful to the reader, and will establish a basic pattern for practical use of the material. As magical arts are essentially a series of highly-effective patterns that generate change, either within or beyond the individual, this opening summary gives an overview of the way in which the patterns are employed in this book.

The key concepts of all western magic are as follows.

1) *The Circle or Wheel of Life:* a fourfold cycle of relationships between energy and consciousness, ranging from the cycle of human growth to the Seasons, or from the Elements to the Stars.
2) *The Four Elements and Four Primal Powers:* Air, Fire, Water, Earth, and Life, Light, Love and Law. These relative terms are human means of coping with energies that run conceptually through all existence.
3) *The Four Worlds:* relative states of manifestation or development which are present in all appearances, from human thought to the appearance of stars and galaxies. These states or modes are: Origination, Creation, Formation, Expression.
4) *The Tree of Life:* a pan-cultural symbol which fuses many

apparently separate philosophical, magical, religious and spiritual concepts into a pattern of relationships. The Tree enables the magician or meditator to establish guidelines during practical work, but on its deeper levels it acts as a metaphysical map of reality.

Each of the four patterns or master-keys listed above is described in detail later; furthermore they are not separate items, but fuse together to form a coherent symbolic guide both to ourselves and to the universe which we reflect. The four patterns are the basics of magical art and related meditative work; they are drawn traditionally as flat plans or maps on paper to help training and study. With practice they soon work as three-dimensional or spherical symbols encompassing the imagination or consciousness; this is their true practical value for magical art. This concept is both simple and profound, for all Being, all consciousness, extends infinitely in all directions. . . the shape generated is a sphere.

Although wordy descriptions can be confusing or even dull, there is nothing in any of the key concepts that is complex or difficult to imagine; most of the illustrations in this book are very direct and simple, and act as guides for our inner visualisation or imagination just as much as they feed information to our intellects. Paradoxically these simple maps or patterns are the most powerful and advanced symbols in magical art; they are never outgrown or abandoned, for they change as the individual develops, and their levels of power and meaning intensify with practice and understanding.

The Tree of Life

The Tree of Life listed above has ten basic units or Spheres in accepted use today; this pattern (shown in Figure 3) is merely one reduced presentation of a series of more complex interrelationships, most of which are not relevant to practical experience and inner growth, but play an important part in the relationship between mysticism, metaphysics and mathematics. In actual practical work, these more complex forms are hardly ever required. Our main text includes ten short chapters which correspond to the ten Spheres or relative modes of energy and consciousness or cosmic manifestation shown upon the Tree of Life. But this is not a book on Hebrew Kabbalah, and not a book on westernised or Christianised Kabbalah.

The Tree of Life has western parallels which predate the appearance of Hebrew mysticism in Renaissance philosophy. Later developments in literature of the eighteenth and nineteenth centuries used very shaky derivations of Hebrew Kabbalah without being aware of the Tree in native magical traditions. The Tree is a map of relationships, or of polarised energies...nothing more or less.

In our ten short chapters based upon the powers or qualities of each Sphere, there is no attempt to list Hebrew attributes. This type of work has been repeatedly published elsewhere, often with no genuine connection to Hebrew mystical cultural roots, and much of it is totally irrelevant to the practice and philosophy of western magic. If, however, you are a Jewish mystic or scholar, there are many profound texts available within genuine spiritual traditions, drawn from Jewish culture through the centuries. Likewise there are profound texts and traditions available for westerners, many of which have been ignored or misunderstood due to orthodox political religious influence upon society. The modern westernised Tree of Life is an excellent example of cross-fertilisation between traditions; it is a pan-cultural symbol.

Our discussion of each Sphere is centred upon the practical and theoretical applications in magical art, particularly for the modern student. Thus the ten short chapters are less concerned with names of angels and incantations than with the actual practice and effect of the qualities and energies of each Sphere in human activity. Each of these ten chapters, however, includes a short list of key attributes. Many of these are not identical to the attributes published in earlier literature which has an overbalanced emphasis upon male gender or masculine principles. Where a feminine symbol or image has been replaced by a masculine one through religious orthodoxy, the balance of polarity of magic is seriously disrupted. This applies particularly to westernised Kabbalah, in which the feminine nature of the Spheres is confused. Where such changes have been identified, the comparisons between the standard much-copied attributes in publication and the primal images or powers are clearly shown in our text. (For readers who wish to pursue the customary lists of attributes found in literary sources, a number of useful books are suggested in the Bibliography.)

The Four Worlds

The Four Worlds demonstrate an ancient and effective model of reality. It is incorporated within the Tree of Life, but exists worldwide as an ancient cosmological and psychological pattern without the refinement of the Ten Spheres and their connecting Paths. The Four Worlds form a vertical axis for our sphere of consciousness, just as they represent a metaphysical axis for the universal sphere of manifestation or development from energy to matter.

The Four Elements and Primal Powers

Just as the Four Worlds (Origination, Creation, Formation, Expression) form a vertical axis or spindle, so do the Four Elements or Powers form the horizontal axis of our magical or cosmological sphere. As the planets, stars and galaxies rotate, so does the total sphere of consciousness. This cyclical spiralling or rotating property of energy is a major feature of magical art in application and practical use.

The Wheel of Life

In our collective human world the vertical and horizontal cycles manifest; the horizontal rotation appears as the Four Seasons and related phases such as human life cycles, while the vertical fourfold pattern appears as the human body, and the associated 'directions' in world-space. They are, of course, up/down or zenith and nadir, while the horizontal cycle defines East, South, West and North. The obvious relativity and regionalising of concepts does not debar them from magical applications; we have moved from metaphysical concepts to the stance of the human body and our orientation upon the planet Earth. This analogy may be applied in reverse for magical work, in which very simple patterns and movements generate highly energised results in terms of consciousness and higher powers of apprehension normally blocked through a conditioned worldview. In other words, the conditioned worldview is used to destroy itself.

The Four Worlds also correspond to power centres (sometimes inaccurately called psychic centres) which are traditionally taught as locations within the body. These locations are sources or nodes of energy which share qualities with four levels of existence. In our solar system these manifest as Stars, Sun, Moon and Earth. Once again this is a simple pattern based upon geocentric observation; but it works nevertheless as our total individual and collective worldview through human time is grounded in such concepts.

The simple maps and harmonic relationships lead to dynamic

6

changes of awareness; they are not merely catch-all systems to satisfy our ignorance.

The Third Ring of the Universal Sphere

There is, of course, a third defining cycle in our theoretical sphere of universal consciousness. This is the centre and circumference of Being, which encompasses all other categories, known and unknown.

In practice, magical art does not consist of worrying unduly about spheres, rings and similar patterns. It does, however, consist of humankind standing upright and relating six basic directions (see Figure 9) to planetary, solar and stellar concepts. Much of this basic theory is developed in our later chapters, with an emphasis upon practical experience rather than intellectual juggling with geometry or proportions.

Tarot Trumps, God or Cosmic Images, Paths of Power

Following the introductory material and the ten short chapters derived from the Tree of Life there is an analysis of the role of Tarot images in magical art. This includes a system of relationships between the Tarot Trumps and the Tree of Life which is virtually unknown in modern publication, yet which merges with the ancient holistic worldview that should be the foundation of modern magical art. Tarot images were originally a form of non-verbal educational symbols, used either in a literal sense for story-telling, or on deeper levels for meditation upon universal qualities. Later corruptions such as idle fortune-telling or juvenile association with 'black magic' and 'diabolism' are directly due to the imbalance introduced by mono-sexual political religion and propaganda.

Innerworld Contacts

Towards the end of the book, a section on Innerworlds and innerworld contacts is found, including some practical exercises in these central concepts of traditional magical initiation. The major premise of magic is that there are many worlds, and that the transformations which occur within the magician enable him or her to gain access to these worlds. While this subject is known world-wide through folklore, fairy tales and wisdom traditions, we are concerned here with a modern restatement of the methods used in magical arts to achieve contact with other worlds and other beings. It must be stressed very strongly that this is not, and never has been, connected to 'spiritualism'. The difference between magical contacts or innerworlds and spiritualism is dealt with in more detail in the relevant chapters.

Examples and Exercises

The reader should first simply read through the whole book, from beginning to end, without attempting the exercises. A more experienced worker may be tempted to by-pass the early chapters, but they contain many items relevant to the more unusual technical and practical exercises found towards the close of the book. The material does not develop in graded sections or lessons, but is spread equally throughout the text, occasionally focusing upon practical work or detailed projects for inner development.

The practical material falls into several categories, the most important of which are a number of short ritual patterns, visualisations, and inner techniques such as defined meditations and dreamwork. Additionally, there are a set of exercises based upon attributes (such as Tarot Trumps and the Paths of the Tree of Life) which are intentionally left incomplete for the reader to develop along lines suggested by the system described.

After reading the entire book, some practical work with the concepts of the Worlds, Directions, and the opening and closing ritual patterns should be undertaken. Following this, the 'Tower and Landscape' exercise, then the methods for establishing innerworld contacts. A major magical task is the personal summary and assembly of the Tarot Trumps and Paths; this work-programme is explained in our chapter on Tarot Trumps, and should be carefully and thoroughly carried out. Once again, it is worth emphasising that this not only a 'beginner's' exercise; it works very effectively for those who have experience of magical work, and complements the more widely published and popularised systems generally taught. As a general rule, the patterns inherent in magical art, such as the Wheel or Circle, the Four Worlds, the Tree and its Paths, amply define a programme of work, training and balanced development.

Origins and Authority

It must be emphasised, immediately, at the beginning of the book, that there is no claim here of 'completeness' or 'authority'. This is not a dictatorial all-inclusive text, and it does not derive from any hierarchical origin or pseudo-mysterious magical order.

Indeed, as an author, I am pleased to say that this text is deliberately incomplete! Any book which offers the reader full detailed totally refined and defined explanations of magic is utterly valueless. The completion of magical art is within ourselves, and not upon the pages of a book.

On a more practical level the exercises, meditations, visualisations and ritual patterns are variants of ancient and enduring formulae which have been known in magical tradition (in various forms) for many centuries. These practical sections are the foundational elements of advanced magic; they may be moved and combined into innumerable cycles and relationships. When such root symbols and ritual elements or patterns are correctly worked, they rapidly lead in to further material and specific developments. In this book, as in oral magical training, the material is often left open-ended; the value lies not in the words themselves but in the work that we do with them. Our examples are not religious texts, and they have no dogmatic or hierarchical weight or value.

A great deal of magical training, even at the most advanced stages, consists of doing things for yourself. With this rule firmly in mind, I have given guidelines for a number of techniques, many of which have not been previously published. It is up to us, collectively and individually, to work with these techniques and move them forward into the magical future. This individual or group effort in drawing up the patterns of magic is a most profound experience that changes consciousness. It is our human reflection and recreation of the origin of all Being, no matter how limited our magical mirror may be initially.

Anyone can comfortably trot out page after page of lists from reference sources; most occultists and would-be-magicians seem to go no further than reading or writing such lists, or quibbling over trivia such as the correct way to light or extinguish a candle or their various personal talents and superiorities. None of this journalistic or petty nonsense has any connection to magical art; it is merely human weakness, laziness or egocentricity reflected through magical interests on the social or hobby level. Similar irrelevant side-tracks are found in any part-time leisure fad or ego-inflating practice. Magic is a total and unrelenting way of life, not a craze or subject for discussion groups.

Once the reader has worked with the practical examples, I would recommend a further reading of the entire book, as many of the concepts in magical art are transformed by practical work. This is the curious quality and property of magic; the same units undergo many significant transformations without losing their primal identity. We could, of course, be cunning and suggest that it is the psychic orientation or understanding of the magician that changes, while the symbols remain constant and eventually become irrelevant. I leave the reader to make his or her own choice between such rationalisations; however we describe it, the method works if it is seriously undertaken.

Methods of Magical Tuition

There are two ways of teaching magic: the first is through careful intellectual explanation followed by guided practice; the second is through direct experience which renders the explanatory material redundant but leaves the regular thought processes struggling to catch up with the new realisations that have occurred. There are countless books on esoteric subjects which follow the first method, while the second method, rare today, is the original traditional way of teaching magical arts. I have attempted to merge the two methods together in this book, hence its departure from many of the standard systems and literary accumulations copied from book to book in occult publication.

If the reader is unsure of or merely bored with the explanatory material, the exercises are ultimately the most important elements in the book. Magic is something which must be done rather than talked or read about.

Magical Traditions and Magical Revivals

To conclude this guide to the reader in his or her practical use of the book, some definition of the type of magic described and developed must be attempted. Although there is much current publicity and commercial development of an 'occult revival', the magical traditions described in the following pages are not part of this type of fashion or craze, either historically or in their content. Strictly speaking, each century has a type of 'occult revival' in which magical arts take fashionable and often ridiculous forms; they are also developed in certain technical directions through original research and scholarly work. Behind these two revivalist themes (popular fashion and intellectual reassessment or research) runs an enduring tradition or cycle of traditions. The relationship between these traditions and their unity in diversity is shown in our Figure 4. Magical arts are supported by a perennial philosophy and ethical tradition; they are intimately linked to spiritual development and in effect magical arts eventually dispose of themselves, for they are means and not ends. The more popular and bizarre practices (which are mainly propaganda or unpleasant fiction), play no part in the magical traditions demonstrated in this book.

In primitive cultures, however, there are many perverted magical practices used for ignorant or selfish ends; no serious student of folklore or anthropology would pretend that all such magic is beneficial or spiritually uplifting. Western magical arts, however, are far removed from such crudities, although modern equivalents are found in spiritualism, so-called 'Satanism' and other unhealthy activities. Anything trivial, time- and energy-consuming, or ultimately sinister should be disposed of by the genuine magician; it can only lead to devolution or imbalance.

The magic offered in the following pages is derived from perennial philosophy and enduring tradition; it comes from myth, legend, visionary cosmology and poetic insight. It does not derive from underground cultism, secret elitist movements or any form of anti-religion. The term 'magic' has frequently been abused and separated from a spiritual foundation; such separation cannot be levelled against magic as a whole any more than the appalling crimes committed in the name of 'God' can be levelled against true faith or religion.

INTRODUCTION

More nonsense has been written about Magic than about any other subject; but this is not surprising as Magic is intimately linked to our imaginations, and those who allow their imaginations to run wildly and freely often write about Magic. *Magic is basically an artistic science in which we control and develop our imagination to cause changes in the outer world.* Nothing more and nothing less. No matter what other techniques, systems, traditions or religions are involved, all magical theories derive from controlled work with the imagination.

Before we take this any further it is worth disposing of some of the more absurd and quite untruthful notions and propaganda still found regarding Magic. Until we throw away a great deal of such dirty bathwater we will not be able to find the simple child from which all human creative and scientific endeavour has matured; all human development be it material or spiritual is due to Magic...it is a magical process in which consciousness causes changes to the world.

1) *Magic is not confined to 'the occult'.* Occultism, the science or study of that which is usually hidden, should not be confused with the generally vague and somehow disreputable subject of 'the occult'. The very term is an indication of its own absurdity, as it literally means 'the hidden' and does not describe any movement or tradition or actual subject matter at all...it is just poor grammar masking confusion and misinformation. *Occult* is derived from an astronomical or astrological event, in which the sun or another heavenly body is occulted or eclipsed, hidden from view by the presence of another planet. An occultist is, or should be, someone who tries to study hidden or obscured subjects and bring them out into the light.

'The occult' conveys the idea of secret groups or elitist individuals chasing after powers which are as fatuous and impossible as the

12

popular image can make them. There are powers in Magic, very potent powers indeed, but they are the common energies and property of all humankind, of all life, and are not part of any shadowy and ignorant conspiracy. There is folly and viciousness in all aspects of life, so it is not in any way a revelation or a profound truth to find that some magical practitioners are fools or egomaniacs or quite totally and utterly mad. They share such personality disorders with politicians, scientists, preachers, doctors and ordinary men and women in all walks of life.

2) *Magic is not inherently evil.* This follows from our first comments about 'the occult', but so much nonsense is attached to the evil and corrupting powers that are supposed to be inherent in magical practices that a separate short statement is necessary. Evil dwells in the individual through imbalance; magic is a neutral set of artistic and scientific techniques for controlling the imagination, the life energies, and the effect of consciousness upon the outer world. Magic might equally re-balance an 'evil' person, just as it might unbalance a weak one. Once we remove Magic from the silly comic-book realm of 'the occult' we find that it embraces all growth and creativity, all scientific development, for all these things come from humankind applying the power of consciousness to the outer world by varying means. Our first steps in the direction of such growth are *magical*, both culturally at the dawn of time, and individually at the beginning of a new life as a tiny child.

The sources for the supposed and unproven 'evil' of Magic are twofold: Propaganda and Fear.

Most of the Propaganda originated with the political Churches, who worked very hard indeed to suppress many aspects of pagan or pre-Christian worship, wisdom, education and traditions regarding the relationship between humankind and the Universe. Much of this propaganda is carried over into the present day, and it all boils down to one thing: control of power over people. We often forget that only a few hundred years ago there was no 'occult', only a varied set of traditions in worship and magical practices which included developing Christianity. As we shall see in later Chapters, even modern Christianity has many *magical* practices which are identical to those of pagan worship from the most ancient times. If magic is evil, in the light of historical evidence, then Christianity must also be evil through its regular and highly organised use of magic. Obviously, this is not the case.

Magic is neutral: evil lives in the imbalance of people who may or may not use Magic to enhance their own false images of themselves.

We shall always proceed from this standpoint in the development of our discussion of Magic.

3) *Magic summons up old outmoded gods and goddesses or demons.* This is a very confused subject indeed, and demands a certain amount of belief or superstition on the part of the accuser. If we add to this popular notion the materialist concept that Magic incites people to believe in otherworld beings, we can consider both suggestions as aspects of one general objection based on both Propaganda and Fear.

We shall be considering the important differences between gods, goddesses and demons (or daemons) in later chapters; for the present summary we can affirm that Magic does indeed awaken aspects of our awareness which are represented by ancient figures or symbols found within both Christian and pre-Christian pagan religions. The same can be said truthfully of many aspects of psychotherapy, while anyone with even a superficial grasp of magical imagery can see such 'god-images' working in a debased and trivialised manner in television commercials, pop music videos and political propaganda. Although such commercial images are trivialised, they are by no means weak, and represent one of the most powerful modern uses of Magic in general society.

In Magic the ancient images are highly refined and tuned, and are employed as focus points for concentration or meditation or as symbolic units for ceremonial use. There is nothing wildly secret about this; it is found in many walks of life without a formal label, and is employed in religion worldwide. The essential difference is that magical traditions use specific images or god/goddess forms, in order to gain specific results with the imagination and its effect upon the outer world. If we struck out the words 'god/goddess' from the previous sentence it could apply to psychotherapy or even to nuclear physics; both use specific images or constructs to gain specific ends. Neither science assumes that systems are ultimate or rigid, and magical systems are equally fluid and subject to development and refinement.

MAGIC AND THE WORLD: LEAVING OR SAVING?

There is a certain amount of confusion in both literature and general tuition concerning magic and the magician's relationship to the consensual or so-called real and normal world. Before taking this matter a step further, we must realise that the 'normal' world is a fiction, a collection of mutually reinforced delusions. We can grasp

14

this hard truth when we see it at work in the deluded worldviews of any people with whom we disagree politically, socially, economically, philosophically, or in religious matters; but we rarely extend such understanding of relative delusion to its full and proper extent, which includes *all* worldviews, not excluding our own. On a scientific level modern studies of perception, conditioning and childhood development go a long way towards redefining truths long established in esoteric traditions regarding consciousness; our patterns of perception are merely shared conveniences, reinforced by repetition and association with other members of groups such as family, society, culture or race.

Modern magicians writing in the twentieth century have made an effort to assert repeatedly that we must not leave the world behind, but that we should transform it. This teaching is merely a restatement of a very ancient mystical truth, but in our modern context it emerged as a corrective to the vapid pseudo-spirituality of various nineteenth-century esoteric movements and societies, who chose to merge a misunderstanding of Eastern mysticism and religion with the pernicious orthodox propaganda that the world is evil, non-spiritual, and to be abandoned as soon as possible in favour of Heaven or some other less substantial realm.

The magician does not seek to flee the world; he or she seeks to transform it. The transformation begins within new directions of awareness sought in early training, but finally it permeates the entire entity through to the physical body; thus is the world abandoned, for it only exists as a consensus of mutual delusions reinforced by habit. In religious terms the world must be *saved*, but the magical traditions, without denying this religious truth, affirm a more subtle aspect of it, that all worlds may be *transformed*. The magician who seeks to run away from the collective world into an imaginative realm is someone who is inseparably tied to that same collective world from which he or she longs to depart. In practical magic, such dreamy escapes are soon found to be difficult for a number of technical magical reasons.

A major part of magical work consists of contacting and entering into other worlds; no magical training or initiation can succeed without such encounters, and they are found at the core of magical traditions worldwide regardless of culture or race. Although the change of worldview begins within the intellect for the western student, or within an active local tradition of belief for the individual in countries where magic is still part of folk culture, it rapidly enters the realm of the imagination, leaving both intellectual and folkloric transition stages behind.

15

For developing magical arts, the imagination is a potent tool available to the student, but it is not an end in itself. The imagination is transformed and re-attuned by a series of holisms or conceptual models, such as those shown in our diagrams, which have a resonant effect upon the psyche and the body. Such holisms may appear as simple symbols, or may be imaginatively recreated as scenes, landscapes, images, or employed in magical ritual by combining the symbolic patterns with intense visualisation and direction of personal and group energies on many levels of awareness including physical movement and bio-electrical responses.

In the enduring magical traditions, as in the religious traditions, there is an advanced stage at which the physical body leaves the consensual world altogether, and is translated to other dimensions. An enormous shift of the direction and patterns of energy is required for this transition, and the mutually reinforced world is left behind. This ancient teaching is no mere trick to vitalise our imagination, it is taught as a sober fact.

Paradoxically, we may not perceive the reality of other worlds, until we have understood the reality of our group-world (the 'real' or consensual world). By unravelling the mutually reinforced delusions we actually unravel the world; it has no other 'reality' that separates it from any other state, dimension, or world emerging from the ground of Being. Here is where magical traditions may differ from mystical or religious ones, for we do not unravel the world seeking to pass directly into the truth of Being, Divinity, or the Unknown. Magical teaching asserts that such attempts cannot be made without prior experience of other worlds, as consciousness needs to experience certain states before it approaches the Unknown. This is definitely not intended as a hierarchical series of advancement, for the worlds encountered vary enormously, and do not necessarily follow a rigid order even within any one cultural tradition.

The law of encountering Worlds may be by-passed, but in so doing we run the risk of dissipating our energies and emerging into a state that is nowhere near Truth but somewhat removed from shared reality. The practical magician avoids such limbo conditions very carefully indeed, relying strongly upon interaction and experiences of alternative states of being or inner worlds.

If we transform ourselves sufficiently through reassembly and redirection of our energies, we experience other worlds. This change of worldview enables us to gain a more accurate picture of the shared or outer world; by leaving it behind, we enter it more fully. Vague dissolution or weakening of a worldview is not encouraged in magic; total reformation is sought instead.

The constant emphasis upon transformation in magical training may enable the adept to affect the outer world, while the magical group may combine energies in ritual to tend and encourage phases of growth within human consciousness at large, even on a planetary level. Such operations must be taken with some caution, for many groups spend fruitless time and energy in imaginative exercises that clearly do not effect such changes even though they may strengthen the group's particular world-delusion. Yet such potential powers of transformation are not an idle theory; many matters of grave concern to modern society were first voiced by magical orders who were able to step slightly ahead of world-time or group-time. Many of the now rigid aspects of the consensual world were originally dynamic archetypes mediated by early astronomers or alchemists and magicians; this is not merely 'evolution' of knowledge, but the magical process by which metaphysical perceptions are crystallised through into the outer world.

Thus we have the seeming paradox by which the magician is trained to leave the regular world and seek other realms of Being, but at the same time encouraged not to abandon the world, but to transform it utterly. On a collective level, whenever a man or woman gains a genuine transaction with another world, the bonds of the regular group-world are loosened for everyone within it. This loosening may be upon a divine or cosmic level, such as that of the great Saviour figures, or it may be upon a very small individual level such as that of the magical adept.

The contemporary alternative to such loosening of the world is plain for all to see; it manifests as conditions of nuclear disaster in which the loosening of bonds is passed directly through physical matter rather than through its true mediating route, which should be the unity of humankind upon the planet.

1 MODERN MAGICAL ARTS

To use the word *modern* connected to the practice of *magic* may seem odd; it demands some explanation, for magic is undeniably one of humankind's most ancient fundamental acts... the origin of all arts and sciences.

Magic relies very strongly on tradition, by which we mean a collective stream of information, education, methods and ethics; none of these are fully written out, even in literate cultures. Originally communal traditions were oral, and magic works best upon this oral level, where it is linked intimately to collective and environmental images shared by cultural groups, though usually in an unconscious manner. Primal examples of this type of magic abound in traditional songs, tales, and ritual folk dramas; but such cultural material is only the surface evidence of deeper rooted magical patterns, symbols and techniques, many of which were refined in early civilisations, and may be rediscovered by modern magicians within a new social and cultural context.

Despite the flood of books on magical, meditational and related subjects (which, if we include psychology, is a very great flood indeed) we cannot combine these books, or even their selected strong points, into a whole entity and say 'this is magic'. The true teaching of magic comes from actual work within a magical tradition, and not from theory or pseudo-authoritarian publication, speculation, or vague 'new age' enthusiasm. Many aspects of a magical tradition may only be understood in magical circumstances, with a carefully adjusted flow of awareness in which our attention is directed inwards towards the roots of consciousness in life, rather than outwards towards objects vested with emotional or intellectual charge and attraction. In more complex or highly-energised magical work, the concentrated awareness may indeed be focused upon external elements, sometimes creating remarkable changes, but only after the inner comprehension and response to these elements has been magically transformed. We shall be dealing with many of the methods by which such changes may be achieved as this book progresses.

Modern magical arts, therefore, are a clarification, a restating of ancient enduring traditions in the context of the twentieth and impending twenty-first centuries. By comparison, the magical practices of the nineteenth century were replete with deliberate obscurity, ignorance, and pompous quasi-religious posturing; yet they only reflected, as such practices frequently do, the ambience of the age or culture in which they were undertaken. Magical arts reflect both the greatest strengths and the most pernicious weaknesses of the time in which they are formalised. Despite the eccentricities and weaknesses of the magical revival which arose during the latter part of the nineteenth century, we still rely heavily upon its material, and much of the scholarship and esoteric theory produced by authors within that general movement has hardly been improved upon by modern popular 'occultists'.

Balancing the rather ponderous and pseudo-hierarchical tone of the Victorian adepts (who drew in depth upon the works of the sixteenth to eighteenth centuries) are the light airy publications of the post-war period of the twentieth century, the so-called 'new age' books. Such works are often casual and frivolous to the degree of being meaningless and misdirected; there are no easy ways to inner growth, no rapid cosy sharing caring methods of meditation, therapy or spiritual insight. So many books, courses and teachers have proposed such easy jolly (often highly commercialised) insights that people are once again becoming sceptical, and equating *all* esoteric theory and practice with the vapid wash of popularised spirituality.

Between the two extremes described, there is a middle way. A fresh assessment of magical techniques, symbols and effects upon the individual and practising group may be attempted, and set out in brief for people to take up and work within themselves. Such a reassessment does not replace or oppose other studies or schools or techniques, it merely supplements them and perhaps clarifies some of the frequently vague or wilfully obscured technicalities of magical arts in daily practice.

It is my personal belief that during the years between the mid-1970s and the present day, there has been a noticeable acceleration of what might be called 'advanced' magical arts; work of this type is an effective reinstating of root traditions, many of which are defined in the chapters which follow. By working with primal material in a clear manner accessible to the modern mind, we by-pass the stagnant backwaters of 'occultism' and rebuild a magical tradition which has been fragmented for a long period of time. Thus we turn around the spiral of related time and consciousness, and emerge upon a higher level, with a better view of the universe which is found both within and without.

Paradoxically the sources for this new upsurge of magical practice and improved understanding have always been readily available in the concentrated form of a few early texts and oral or inner imaginative traditions; it may seem strange that they have not been revived or reassessed before, but this paradox is what makes such work magical. That which is obvious, unhidden, *un-occult*, suddenly declares its presence, shining with a transformative light. The occultation has been within ourselves both individually and collectively. The dramatic negative cultural changes that have swept across the western world in the wake of developing technology have been paralleled by changes in the general consciousness, changes which manifest in small groups or individuals as a heightened awareness of spiritual cognition, or a genuine practice of creative magic. This marriage of apparent opposites, of gross materialism and spiritual insight, is an expression, on a broad scale, of one of the fundamental and primary laws of magic; spiritual principle is utterly present in material practice. It is only our limited and padlocked consciousness that does not grasp this potent truth. The truth itself exists nevertheless, and may be realised through the enduring artistic disciplines of creativity, or through meditation and magical ritual.

Contrary to popular fantasy, magical arts are not employed to 'get what you want', but to unlock whatever you are not, thus revealing or releasing whatever you may be.

With each phase of culture in history, the locks upon our consciousness have changed their form or expression, but in essence remain the same. Certain locks are contrived from willed patterns of suppression, control, propaganda, sexual stereotyping, religious dogma; these combine with and reinforce the old familiar locks restraining individual awareness; laziness, greed, self-interest, and, most pernicious of all, wilful ignorance. This last negative quality is the most difficult of all to transform into a positive; if we truly will ourselves to be ignorant, and most of us do in ways ranging from the most trivial to the most appallingly irresponsible and culpable, then transformation comes only through bitter experience. It may seem to be hardship imposed from without, almost at random, but magical tradition suggests that it flows from our own deepest levels of energy, which, denied valid expression by the locks upon our consciousness, find an outlet through exterior cause and effect.

Magical techniques remove the locks, permanently, and often with surprising or even drastic effect. Any genuine teacher of meditation or magical work will begin to reveal this fearful element as early as possible to the student; if this is not done, the teacher is lying or cheating, or simply does not truly know the subject that he or she claims to teach. In other words any method or teacher who does not deal with the disturbing effects of magic and meditation upon the coagulated rigid outer personality is a fraud.

In some cases methods of tuition that offer easy insight or group support and a sense of righteous belonging are actually deliberate and pernicious methods of suppression, leaving us trapped in a cosy pool of pseudo-emotion and debilitating energetic interactions. The magical traditions are surprisingly strict in this context of what is and is not acceptable for the student; tradition would advise against our widespread and popularised meditational cults, all types of regression, hypnosis, and sensitivity training for apparently 'psychic' purposes, evangelical cults that parade spiritual elitism or fervent enthusiasm, mutated eastern religions grafted upon western audiences or participants, and the host of vague but energy-consuming 'new age' techniques, offerings, gatherings, festivals, psychic or mental therapies (particularly) and meetings.

What, the reader might ask, is left? Curiously, the magical traditions do not, contrary to the fantasies of pulp fiction or journalism, decry or oppose the great religions, by which we mean the genuine religions working in their own cultural context. There is no clash between magical tradition and the various branches of Christianity, Buddhism, Islam, Hinduism, or any of the established lines of spiritual nourishment or formalised worship. Not, at any rate, from the viewpoint of the magician, although orthodox religions have often persecuted and banned magical arts in long-standing attempts to secure sole possession of keys to the padlocks, or the keys to heaven itself. If you feel that magical arts are not for you, that mysticism is too difficult, but you require a system of spiritual expression, then a true religion, with its great imaginative traditions and ritualised dramas, is still a valuable medium for the individual to use to relate to whatever Reality lies behind the expressed images of God or Goddess.

Those who truly wish to persist with magic, which is to undertake an artistic science that transforms consciousness, have a deep inner requirement to reach beyond the limitations of formal religion or conditioned materialism, to seek the truth hidden within illusion.

THE RELATIONSHIP BETWEEN FAITH, WORSHIP AND MAGIC

There is often confusion over the relationship between magic and faith (belief in an ultimate Being or Deity), and magical ceremony and worship. If we were to ask whether or not magic involves faith and worship, the answer would be yes, but not in the general or popular meaning of the words employed. Magic is a practical art, sometimes it is called a craft (though this is confused nowadays with popularised witch-craft); it is something which is *done* rather than theorised, looked at, or read about. Magic may only be understood through active participation, and its results may not and cannot be bought or sold. In this sense it is possible for people to work magical rituals without belief in a deity, originator or creative consciousness ...but such magical work is limited, as it cannot extend far beyond the self-imposed limits of its originators. We may find degraded magic of this sort daily in television commercials, political speeches, pop-videos and other sources that seek to apply emotive ritualised patterns to the malleable imagination of our culture at large, or to specifically selected segments of the consumer population.

This limitation of magic, established by the boundaries of the imagination of the operator in the first instance, is an extremely important magical law. The effect of magic is limited according to your own belief and understanding of reality; so rigid is this law that it may be stood upon its head by the experienced magician to prove that understanding of reality is only limited according to the effect of magic.

What must be emphasised in this context is that we are dealing with the genuine or true beliefs of the individual or group; what we assume we believe, what we think is our understanding of reality, and what we actually do believe, are often radically different or even contradictory to one another. One of the effects of magical training is to fuse these two levels of belief and understanding into one balanced conceptual model...a model that is open-ended and without specific limits.

During the early stages of magical development and training, in which the individual is often emerging from a period of scepticism or anti-religion, this conflict is very apparent. The law of belief in magic is not merely a matter of auto-suggestion, credulity, or self-reinforced delusion; it runs far deeper than such superficial manifestations. In old-fashioned terminology it is one of the great secrets of the universe, taught as 'be what thou wilt, if thou knowest thy will truly'. Our history is full of sciences, achievements, even empires, built upon systems, practices and beliefs now known

22

to be false, yet such systems worked very well indeed for those who believed in them. This was not due to delusion on the part of the believers, but because the power of belief is more potent and active than the object or system believed in. Expressions or forms change ceaselessly, but consciousness is eternal, and has an enduring seed of stillness at its core.

Because of the practical nature of magic an effective magician does not speculate upon the nature and requirements of deity, contrary to psychological and anthropological opinions about magic. Any magician at any time in history soon discovers that deity or Being exists in countless aspects, images, forms and patterns. All such expressions derive from a whole or harmonic consciousness that permeates the universe. Quibbles over the gender or will of god or goddess are for the limited political religions; magic attempts to relate human consciousness to divine consciousness through patterns inherent in each. There is little more to the art of magic than that attempt; the rest is mere technique[1]. (See Bibliography.)

Worship is less obvious in magical rituals than in religious rituals. It is not a major aim of magical tradition to congregate and praise Divinity or to utter prayers and petitions; such needs are or should be fulfilled adequately by the religious organisations of the magicians' own culture.

The element of sheer worship, like that of belief in Divinity, is actually taken for granted in magic, though not in any flippant manner. Any generation of a holistic pattern, any act that opens an imaginative gate between the worlds, is, by its very nature, an act of worship. In such an act, the worshipper realises that he or she is in the presence of an awareness, being, or power that epitomises and transcends the beliefs of the celebrant; magic cannot work without belief in a unified universal consciousness. Praising god as a vague means of extracting response to personal desires is not sufficient; true worship is the result of experience, however fleeting, of a divine presence, of a power that realigns regular directions of attention, a presence that indicates a new and yet eternal reality.

Revival pagan cults have a powerful motivation towards goddess worship. They act as a corrective to rebalance the bizarre mono-sexual image of deity that has been sustained for several centuries by political Christianity. Magical tradition in general, however, tends to advise against limited worship of specific god-forms to the exclusion of any others. In ritual or imaginative visualisation such forms are employed as focusing devices for energies; no matter how autonomous they appear inwardly (and some of them have degrees of autonomy far exceeding average human imagination) they are still limited by the form and function that they express. God or goddess forms are working images structured, as it were, out of the sensitive malleable energies of the imagination, engineered to a high standard of performance. If they were not so, unmediated or untransformed energies would damage the consciousness of the ritualist or visualiser; this fact is well stated in myths concerning the inadvisability of mortals to look upon the face or body of the Goddess or the love-making of the gods.

The magician passes through and beyond such images without ever denying or degrading their validity. Ultimately magic aims at an apprehension of reality that transcends imagery, but which energises the old god-forms, including those found in world religions.

Despite exotic theories at one extreme and intellectual rationalisation at the other, magic is still founded upon the premise that consciousness is illimitable and consubstantial with all phenomena. In general terms this means our consciousness is shared not only with other human beings, but with all living creatures and with so-called inanimate expressions of energy and matter. This is not because magicians are stupid people who think that stones are cosy stereotypes of humans, much as sentimental people do with pet animals, but because of a resonant intuitive perception which predates modern physics by millennia, yet is in keeping with the most modern theories of the relationship between matter and energy. This intuition, which has been the foundation of esoteric teaching through the ages, is that all existence is made up of energy at relatively different rates of vibration or resonance, forming complex sets of relationship; ranging from matter through to biological life forms and on to radiant energies of stellar origin.

Magical art demonstrates this truth in various ways, employing systems or holisms of symbols that act directly to transform consciousness. With the important proviso that students must attempt to understand ancient systems only in proper cultural context, we can state that magical psychology has always been with us as a genuine wisdom or science; modern materialist psychology is merely a limited re-statement of certain areas already well known and publicised in magical systems. Certain modern schools such as psycho-synthesis are drawn almost verbatim from the visualisation and polarity techniques known to both east and west for many centuries in the context of meditation, magic and transcendant consciousness[2].

Magical art, however, is more than psychology; it embraces physiology, bio-electrical theory and practice, higher modes of awareness not admitted into modern psychological theory, and

ultimately aims at a symbolic entry into the realms of stellar existence, physics and metaphysics, via finely tuned and specific altera-
tions of awareness. None of the above is in any way new or unusual,
such areas are the known properties of magic through various manifestations or schools in each century or culture.

Physiology is found in ritual, dance, drama, the martial arts and
yoga, while bio-electrical theory and practice are integrated with
controlled diet, environment and polarisation of the sexual energies.
This polarisation plays a major role in the health and the inner
disciplines of the dedicated mystic and magician. It is found in
scientific systems such as alchemy, and in the orthodox churches in
various, albeit odd, practices regarding sensuality which are now
little understood. The stellar expression of magic is at its most
popular with astrology, which was originally a system of synchron-
ised magical astronomy, and not primarily intended to establish
character or psychic trends for individual horoscopes.

Magic is, therefore, a holism of various arts and sciences
integrating aspects of consciousness. The patterns and symbols
employed are not mere superstition, but are derived from factual
experience; today's fact is tomorrow's superstition, and discarded
scientific systems abound in cultural history. Yet such systems often
hold the seeds of esoteric practices and deeper levels of meaning.
Because a system is abandoned or even disproven by current science
does not mean that it is invalid or worthless, merely that we have
superseded certain practical aspects, merging new practices with a
new set of what will in time also become superstitions. Magical arts
are inevitably the forerunners of the science of the future, even if the
materialisation of the science concerned is hostile to its magical
forebear.

There is no suggestion that gross superstition is comparable to the
intentional disciplines of genuine magic; the first is a collective,
random and often vicious outlet for ignorance and fear, while the
second is a coherent set of traditions regarding human potential.

The most obvious example of magical art preceding scientific
expression is the enduring theory that energy and consciousness are
found in so-called inanimate objects. This is now a scientific fact, at
least as far as the concept of energy is concerned, and in the nuclear
age it is our cultural nightmare. Yet the concept of energy in matter
is central to magic, even of the most crudely primitive sort beloved
by anthropologists and psychological reductionists. In refined
systems found in ancient cultures, or the curious pan-cultural blend
of the middle-ages in alchemy and metaphysics, the qualities of
human consciousness were repeatedly compared to stellar patterns,

25

with correspondences right through into the plant and mineral worlds. Energy was, in short, known to be inherent in all existence. It remained for modern physics to liberate this energy in a material realm, where it can only be destructive and poisonous. The energy itself is neutral, but put it in the wrong dimension and it does untold harm; we cannot tap stellar energy on earth without paying an extremely high price. The correct mediation of such energies is through consciousness within the human entity, rather than directly through the destruction of universal matter.

ANSWERS QUESTIONED

The enthusiastic beginner tends to assert confidently that magical arts have all the answers to human problems, even to the secrets of the universe. Unfortunately this attitude is also the hallmark of the fraud and charlatan who seeks to draw money or other less obvious benefits from gullible customers. Popular books on 'new age' magic or meditation, meetings, festivals, courses and seminars all glow with a sense of new-found rightness very similar in its gloss to the righteousness of the evangelical convert. The same enthusiasm is found in those who discover the rightness or leftness of politics, or the reductionism of psychology.

In magic, the brash sense of discovery is often founded upon an old lie, that hidden powers, superiority, secret knowledge and elitist security are all available to the magician. Such desires are human weaknesses; the list given above applies also to rulers or would-be rulers of the world.

What actually occurs with effort and discipline in magical art is something very different from such simplistic imbalanced fantasies. Firstly, magic provides one potential system or framework for the confusion of general consciousness; it is not the only possible framework, and there are many sub-systems in magical traditions. Such means of ordering and eventually re-ordering our perceptions and modes of awareness are particularly relevant to modern society, which is extremely destructive to the individual and collective psyche. The patterns found in magic were less startling to earlier cultures in which religion, family, work and social endeavour were related to seasonal and environmental cycles.

Modern magic correctly places emphasis upon establishing a new relationship with the seasons, the land, the planet, but it does not stop once a degree of such holism has been achieved. Ancient

26

traditions of magic and mysticism were designed to liberate the initiate from the Wheel, which is the cycle of the seasons or the cycle of birth, life, death and rebirth. The modern student or adept must carry the environmental aspects of the art through until they merge with transpersonal, planetary, solar and ultimately stellar modes of awareness. The magical symbols employed are in a state of constant harmonic transformation, uttering octaves or higher harmonics of our first understanding of them, yet remaining true to archetypical matrices. As our consciousness opens, so do the symbols release their power of transformation. The pattern repeatedly found in magic worldwide flows through Earth, Moon, Sun and Stars; each level or world is a phase of a cycle, which may be shown in the model form of a spiral or the Tree of Life.

When individuals discover that it is not, after all, too difficult to realign the regular Earth-based consciousness within themselves, and to seek beyond it for a Lunar or even Solar quality of awareness, there is a tendency to assume that this transformation is the 'answer' to human ills and sorrows. Anyone working with magical arts regularly will know that, paradoxically, the questions are transformed, rather than answers appearing magically.

Magic does not answer questions, it questions answers. At each presumed stage of magical development, a new cycle arises, containing the same questions in higher forms. This is why magical instruction has always been oral, coming from practice and example rather than through correspondence courses or books. The student must experience the transformation of questions within himself or herself, and not demand answers from a set of lessons or a falsely hierarchical teacher acting in a stereotypical manner.

The maxim of the Mysteries was and is 'Mankind know thyself'; this central direction is shared by all mystical, magical and religious traditions or philosophies. Some religions, be they divinely or materially orientated, have wilfully corrupted and concealed this sole instruction that leads towards truth; much of the vilification of magic arises from such vested interests, which run through into modern society with full strength, no matter what shape they appear in, religion, politics, even entertainment.

If you seek magic because you want answers to questions, liberation from personal problems, or power over others, you are likely to have some bitter experiences. Many people simply give up when they find that their illusions are not made more concrete through magic, but are to be utterly shattered along with every pre-conceived self-image and gratifying personal melodrama. Others prefer to remain in the cosy niche of 'occultism' where mysterious powers are hinted at, but never revealed, and answers are always known, but never put into action.

Magic is an art that is generated from questions; there is a consistent mythical pattern in which a god, goddess or otherworld being asks questions of the initiate. Hermes is the traditional patron of magical work, and his image summarises the various questioning deities worldwide; some are kindly and educational, but others are terrifying and shattering. The magician may come to know answers to many riddles, but also to know that there are innumerable questions which may never be answered in the literal sense. Understanding of this type is the converse of the popularised image of occultism, in which vaguely impure or evil secrets are the jealously retained property of furtive power-crazy magicians, slaves to 'the occult'.

On a deeper ethical level, individuals or groups who claim to know all answers to all questions are invariably rigid, inflexible, potentially suppressive or destructive. This applies equally to teachers and students; it is sadly apparent in evangelical sects or pseudo-Eastern cults with strong commercial interests. Why, we might ask, does an inner certainty, a faith or belief or even a revelation generate such aggression and destruction, or at best, such exclusivism? The answer is that beyond the false certainty lives true spiritual awareness; it arises as the intuitive knowledge that nothing is certain, all things transform, even truth.

Here is where the magical path, like that of the mystic, is most hard and unpalatable for many otherwise competent people. The magician must constantly face experiences where he or she plunges into the unknown; occult sciences cannot truly prepare us for this experience, they can only offer general guidance from tradition. Magical training strengthens us to cope with our inner reactions to magical transformation. An analogy to sport may be loosely drawn here, for training keeps the body fit, but cannot replace or simulate the actual race or game which is always a unique unrepeatable experience. Each new step taken in magical art is a step into new realms of consciousness, not a recapitulation of familiar answers.

This seeming paradox is found in one of our oldest and most profound texts of western magical and spiritual enlightenment, Geoffrey of Monmouth's setting out of the *Vita Merlini*[3]. Superficially this is a biography of Merlin's adult adventures, a medieval text drawn from earlier Celtic oral traditions and classical mythology and cosmology. But the *Vita* actually consists of a series of questions that are given most unusual answers, each answer being a nest of

28

questions in itself. Merlin asks all the hard questions that torment us: why is there death, why pain, why love, why do the seasons change and mankind suffer? The answers come in the form of profound cosmic visions, as cruel experiences that burn away personality, even sexuality, revealing that the human cycle is a lesser harmonic of a great cycle, and that the answers required must be opened out into further and more significant questions.

When Merlin finally attunes to the powers of life and death that flow through all creation, he firmly refuses to act as a mentor to the princes of the world, for he cannot answer their problems in any way that would satisfy them (for they are asking the wrong questions). Instead he withdraws to a stellar observatory, with a set of companions, already delving into the next cycle of answers to be questioned, knowing that true wisdom is found both within and beyond the human reference framework.

Magic does not answer questions, but it may enable the questioner to find answers within himself or herself, and to relate those inner answers to the greater patterns of the universe. For every question answered there is an answer questioned.

2 THE BASIC UNITS OF MAGIC

There is little doubt that most of the instructional material found in publications that deal with magic or 'the occult' is superfluous. Obscure bulky volumes and 'secret' systems are really nothing more than the literary contrivances of their authors; they are, in short, the periphery of the magical arts. Beyond this peripheral literature there is an even more obscure and trivial region, in which spiritualism, mediumship, commercial clairvoyance and fortune-telling lurk... the refuse of the magical arts, devoid of clarity or philosophy, fused with ignorance and superstition. Yet many individuals pass through these murky, slightly unhealthy regions; some remain trapped in them.

The relatively unimportant nature of literary occult output is sometimes overlooked in the modern revival; Victorian or early twentieth-century works are regarded as being authoritative rather than topically representative of their culture, class origin, and religious conditioning. Within these limitations some remarkable work was indeed undertaken, and many new works on occult theories are merely derivations of early studies. Some of our modern books are the product of desk, scissors and paste, rather than of the heart, meditation and magical experience. We have a whole class of 'magical' journalists who select, summarise and condense material from a range of early publications, particularly those by colourful powerful individuals or groups. This rash of journalism is essentially pointless and misleading; it bears the same relationship to magical arts as tabloid newspapers bear to the works of Shakespeare, or the lyrics of a pop song to the poetry of William Blake.

The basics of magical arts are sparse and direct; they are known worldwide, though forms of expression will vary from culture to culture. The basic units of magic are natural properties of consciousness. We could express this as a key phrase: *The basic units of magical art are derived from properties of consciousness.*

It is possible to argue that any selected unit, symbol, token or even any phenomenon is the result of properties of consciousness, but in magic the concept is pursued inwardly...towards the roots of consciousness, rather than outwardly in dispute or philosophy and logic regarding the relationship between consciousness and perception of events or objects.

The properties of consciousness employed in magical symbolism are fundamental to existence, be it mineral, human or stellar. To achieve this unified vision or representation of consciousness we cannot use words or pictures alone. Although magical symbols often appear as images or pictures with correspondences or descriptive visualisations, they also have some remarkable properties which enable us to use the most primary keys or glyphs or symbols right through into the advanced stages of perception and magical transformation. These advanced stages cannot be accurately represented by words or pictures; the linguistic or visual symbols are merely a way of approaching such modes of consciousness.

As the magician progresses with the art, certain symbols may be set aside, but basic symbols transform while remaining within their own identities; the transformations are not, of course, in the symbols, but in the perception of the magician. If we consider the attributes of magical implements we can see some good examples of this type of transformation; the implements of Sword, Rod, Cup and Shield are *relative modes of consciousness*, which manifest in the outer world as artifacts, either symbolic as in concentrated magical work, or operational within any construct, action or movement of will. A *Rod* may be the principle of light rays in physics, a length of wooden material, a phallic emblem, a plant or any controlled act of conscious will...plus many human acts that are normally unconscious such as biological functions or processes of awareness. We isolate and identify such rod-functions through selecting them and relating them to other functions. The relativity is usually random in everyday life, but in magic is first summarised and later controlled by the use of symbols such as the Circle or Wheel, the Square, the Triangle, and the more complex Tree of Life. Each of these symbols is dealt with in our various chapters, and they appear as diagrams. In advanced magical arts the symbols are often shown in new dimensions of perception, where they take forms that are not possible to represent through diagrams, models or literary descriptions. The magician's training in the basic expressions of the symbols enables his consciousness to remain in balance and to find a relative anchoring point when such modes of perception arise. In other words, we may move a long way beyond that which is normally called 'occultism' through a set of simple basic properties and symbols that transform our consciousness; this is a matter of discipline and experience rather than literature or journalism.

In the enduring traditions, magical symbols are expressions of properties of consciousness inherent in innumerable orders, categories, worlds or worldviews. They are not rigid, definitive or hierarchical; they are fluid, resonant, harmonic, holistic, and, in the true sense of the word, organic.

Because of this universal quality in which consciousness ranging from the most advanced to the most torpid may be shown through a simple set of symbols, the higher rates or transcendent modes of awareness may be brought through the symbols into the restricted outer world. This outer world is initially the psyche of the magician, and by generating the symbols within the psyche and merging them with its inherent patterns, it is ultimately possible to transform the group environment, which includes both psychic and physical manifestation. To put it simply, magic begins by changing yourself, but eventually it changes the whole world if enough selves partake of it.

The ridiculous popular notion of magic rests upon this type of premise, for it presumes incorrectly that the symbols act upon the outer world without first transforming the consciousness of the magician. The main, indeed the only, real function of magical symbols is to transform the magician. This is our second key phrase for reference: *The function of magical symbols is to transform the magician.*

Without this transformation, we simply cannot progress into magical ability, for magical arts use consciousness as their material. This can be expressed as a diagram (Figure 1), though the diagram in this case is not a master-symbol but merely an aid towards our analysis and its understanding. In our illustration the attention (of an individual or group) is moved *inwards* through ritual, meditation or visualisation; it moves towards, and sometimes attains, a point or realm or state of unified consciousness, which transcends relative differences of any set of perceptions or objects. From this state, the attention is then redirected *outwards*.

The outer world, however, is transformed; initially by changes in the consciousness of the initiate, but ultimately through to the literal transformation of physical expression shared by all humankind, and all other planetary life forms. This may seem a mystery at first, but magic seeks to do in a timeless instant that which is encompassed by

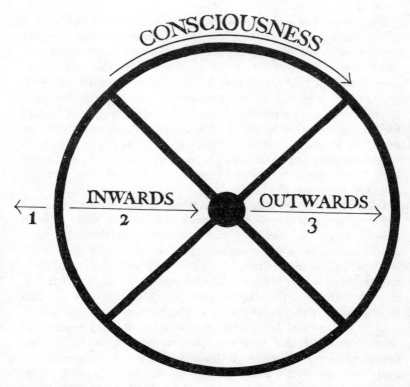

Figure 1. Direction of Awareness. Traditionally the psyche, human conscious energy, is conceived as Four Modes of a sphere (the Powers, Elements, Implements, Seasons, Ages as reflected in a human entity). This totality moves through a relative cycle of change in the course of a lifetime. In magical arts the cycle is intentionally suspended and realigned.
1) Customary conditioned outer direction of awareness at any phase of the cycle.
2) Magical arts turn awareness inwards towards its natural centre. The techniques are taught as the Five Fundamental Arts.
3) Continued work directs awareness from a central balance to return to outer focus in a transformed mode. Perceptions of the world are clarified and rearranged.

history or evolutionary theory over immense time cycles. A transformed consciousness enlivens and changes the psychic and organic elements of the whole entity or being (this much is asserted even by materialist psychology and medicine though it has been known and taught in the transcendent traditions for millennia). Magic may commence with a separation and re-categorisation of parts, but it proceeds to a transcendant unity; this unity is then carried into areas of intent and awareness that are not usually accessible to our limited habitual personalities.

One of the perennial problems with magical work is that it is verbally complex but practically simple. Reams of published matter do no more than attempt to express that which may be grasped fully in a few moments of meditation or ritual work. For this very reason, some of the practical exercises in this book are deliberately left open-ended; the magician is encouraged to make his or her own conclusions and completions. This is the opposite of the literary method of occultism in which thousands of words are wasted on repetitive lists and 'complete' systems; in truth the only magical fulfilment and completion is within ourselves, it cannot exist, by its very nature, upon the printed page. Magic is something which is *done* rather than read about.

In ritual work, for example, a script may seem complex; briefing a group upon its operation sometimes makes it seem more difficult than it really is. Because magic works from deep levels of consciousness, from which verbal expression derives or devolves, it is simpler to undertake the visualisation, perform the ritual, enter into the meditation. Once this has been done, words are obviated; they are useful after the magical event, but redundant before it. This type of work is particularly alien to the modern mind, for we are used to endless and often fruitless discussion of every vagary and twist of an issue; this tendency becomes corrupt to the ultimate degree when we sit around in discussion or encounter groups and deal frivolously with our own patterns of awareness. As in all things, a balance must be struck between narcissistic self-reflection or group mutual gratification, and the extremes of overbalanced solitary will, or group elitism.

In magical tuition there are two general ways of teaching; the first and most recent, which is also the most frequently encountered, is that of explaining everything in carefully graded lessons which advance in degree and intensity as the student develops. The second, more traditional and certainly most primal ancient method is to plunge the student headfirst into a series of direct experiences and to allow the intellect to catch up, sometimes years after the magical events which it cannot at first assimilate.

For modern magical arts, a combination of these two methods is usually the best, but with our increasing cultural tendency to rely upon specialist exposition and lengthy discourse, and our merito-cratic conditioning in which 'grades', 'degrees' and 'qualifications' have acquired a quite spurious glow of charm and validity, perhaps a reversal to the more direct methods of magical tuition would be more effective.

The enduring paradox of magic, which is only resolved by

practical experience and not by words or detailed writing, is repeatedly found in esoteric traditions worldwide. The most valuable thing in the world, they tell us, is all around, yet we cannot see it. In alchemy, the ubiquitous Philosophers' Stone of transformation was made from dung, and was known not to the great scholars, but to humble washerwomen and husbandmen. Magic consists of worlds full of woods, rather than of millions of individual trees.

Another key-phrase may be defined here: *Magic refines many parts into wholes or holistic units without ever losing the parts.* This apparently simplistic phrase will bear considerable fruit in meditation.

PATTERNS AND SYMBOLS

The universal symbols of magic are often the basic symbols of geometry; the keys to earth-measurement. In early culture magic and geometry were identical, and were further related to a cosmic topology or map of universal consciousness expressed as stellar reality. Although this type of holism is no longer used in modern mathematics, it is still valid and fruitful in magical practice. We do not need to move far beyond the most basic, fundamental geometry and mathematics; more sophisticated calculations and formulae abound in magical arts, but as specialist sciences (such as astrology, numerology, gematria and other studies which have been grossly deformed by over-popularisation and ignorance) which are not essential to initiation.

All complexities are derived from powerful and fundamental truths about the relationship between energy and consciousness, Being and matter. Magic uses these truths to transform the innumerable patterns that derive from the basic roots. This is merely another way of saying that magical symbols transform the magician, who then transforms the world.

INITIATION AND 'GRADES'

Nineteenth-century magical societies or orders were strongly influenced by concepts found within the ancient Mysteries (such as those of Egypt, Greece, Rome) and the hierarchical worldview that permeated orthodox political Christianity for several centuries. As a result of this pan-cultural heritage, modern magical arts still retain a rather unfortunate emphasis on 'grades' or pre-defined levels of initiation and hierarchical segregation. This emphasis is gradually fading away in the light of actual experience, for despite a number of literary traditions that assert graded stages of inner development, this is not a feature of true magical development.

Here is yet another paradox; in formal tuition such as classes or published texts, a serial progression (from beginner to experienced) is generally taught. In some groups the emphasis on hierarchical authority (usually vested in a senior male) is strong; as a result most of the members are weakened and deprived of true magical experience, they merely ride along with and support a solo performer or small inner group. This is certainly not adequate for the true magician, who like all magical individuals in folk traditions worldwide must experience for himself or herself. Despite this enervating group practice of graded, authoritarian, carefully doled-out lessons, actual magic never works in a step-by-step manner.

Any genuine teacher will be the first to admit that in magical art (or any related inner discipline) the merest beginner may fly further at times than the most experienced adept; there are no grades or rules that govern the eternal spirit. Teachers who attempt to sit upon the development of their pupils frequently lose the best co-workers, and one of the educational experiences for both 'teacher' and 'pupil' is the breaking down of such stereotypical barriers.

The paradox is really one connected to literacy and social organisation, neither of which play important roles in actual magical traditions. Regardless of an apparent serial or linear tendency within tuition upon paper or in intellectual dissection, magic works by direct experience, and true magical initiation is an open-ended and undefined experience. Once the group or teacher has opened the way for initiation (either in the form of a ritual or an inner experience or through other modes of awareness isolated for specific purposes) there is no limit, barrier or rule that forces the initiate to go only as far as the teacher might wish. Good teachers have no restrictive attitude towards students, and never play superiority games; in magical arts the opening of awareness is experienced and welcomed, not predefined and/or limited. In practice this emerges as the pupil is flung into the deep sea of inner experience and asked to swim; the teacher's greater ability is used only if the pupil sinks, and not to hold him or her back from diving deeper or floating further to the horizon.

Although *explanations* of magical arts are generally divided and graded due to the nature of our verbal/literary communication, *experience* occurs in highly-energised concentrated bursts, which may take years to decode into serial outer awareness.

3 THE FIVE FUNDAMENTAL ARTS

There are five fundamental activities in living magical arts; these persist through the enduring traditions into modern context, and are not likely to be superseded or replaced for a very long time indeed. Within these five there are further sub-divisions and combinations of all five or various aspects of any combination or selection may occur or be required for specific purposes. Although each of these disciplines of consciousness may be developed in relative isolation from the others, they do, in fact, merge together harmonically in any well balanced magical work or specific ritual. *The Five Fundamental Arts* of consciousness are so called because they direct and encapsulate specific modes of energy that are usually random or naturally chaotic within ourselves. In other words, the wide spectrum or power of consciousness itself is given a fundamental form or shape, through specific practices. Into such forms life energies pass, but there is more than this ordering of energies into formal patterns; the attuning process enables the human being to become consciously aware of realms, states, or actual beings that are normally closed to our everyday perception.

In sensitive or visionary people, such paranormal states of awareness arise as intuitions, dreams or waking insights and visions; we all experience psychic events of this sort, though most people choose to forget them or ignore them. In the creative artist or the inventive scientist, the intuitive material is expressed through a specific skill and discipline, either as shape, words or music, or as a formula, theory or concrete function of invention. In the magical arts a selective applied system, traditionally upheld over long periods of time and outer cultural change, refines consciousness into a fine and powerful instrument of transformation and mediation. The first four categories on our list below are primarily means of transformation, be it of the individual, the environment, or the collective image

37

of the world. The fifth category is the response, the counterpoint, or the balancing mode of consciousness for the other four. *These properties of consciousness run through each and every one of us without exception;* but only in the magical arts are they defined and methodically refined as fundamental harmonious practices in their own right.

The five fundamental arts are:

1) Concentration.
2) Meditation.
3) Visualisation.
4) Ritual pattern making.
5) Mediation.

The five fundamentals are listed in a general developing order of importance, but this is not inflexible or intended as a definitive work plan for magical growth. In training (which never ceases) the importance or value of each of our first four disciplines will vary at different stages of development. No one ever reaches a stage where he or she cannot mature through effort with these disciplines.

In early training, we could commence with either *visualisation* or *concentration,* and this depends to a certain extent upon the general characteristics of the individual concerned; *ritual pattern making* is a constant that persists from the most basic to the most advanced levels of magic. In art it is found as creative work, in the generation of music, literature or visual forms; while drama is very close indeed to the magical rituals from which it devolved. In the sciences *ritual pattern making* is expressed as development of artifacts or technologies that appear in the outer world and change our modes of life accordingly.

RITUAL IN PSYCHOLOGY, MAGIC AND FOLKLORE

Before progressing with our analysis, some comment must be made upon the use of the term 'ritual' in psychology and sociology, as this is different in many ways from the original meaning of the word, and tends to confuse our understanding of the magical value of ritual itself. Magical traditions equate both art and science with ritual pattern making; they are inner processes manifesting as outer designs or form; these forms are transformed, purified or modified by the human awareness that brings them through into manifestation. In all such cases there is conscious awareness, will and discipline.

Most of the human individual and social activities defined as 'ritual' in psychology or sociological studies are unconscious, or due in extreme cases to mental imbalance or maladaptive behaviour. In this sense 'ritual' has become almost, but not entirely, a derogatory or reductionist term for 'unreasonable' or compulsive behaviour. There is a great deal of difference between this application of the label 'ritual' and the precise use of the word in the context of creative pattern-making that leads to a material expression.

Linking these two extremes of definition is the *folk ritual* or traditional ceremony, in which magical patterns are collectively expressed without conscious analysis or intellectual interpretation. While such ceremonies form the coherent element in many cultures worldwide, they are disappearing from western culture very rapidly, leaving us without a collective medium to express deep inner needs or statements of shared life.

The folk rituals of the west are, or were, those known to humankind worldwide, but with a natural connection to the culture and locality in which they are enacted. They are not only ceremonies such as genuine sword or Morris dancing, or the death-resurrection plays which are found all over Europe and derive from ancient pre-Christian sources, but situations where people gather to sing, play music, tell stories, or enact certain customary patterns connected to social functions (birth, marriage, adulthood, death). These last patterns may or may not be connected to an orthodox religion[4].

In all of the cases listed above, religious or not, such folk-rituals are being eroded and replaced by entertainment substitutes, mainly in the form of television. The increasing violence of group rituals such as football matches is not merely a reflection of economic or social failure on the part of governments, but of our desperate need for ritual pattern making, a need that cannot be fulfilled; the dynamic energies erupt violently rather than flow naturally through communal or individual paths.

In magical work, ritual pattern making is drawn from ancient and enduring techniques. These techniques represent the most refined and flexible methods of expressing our energies through patterns that give results in the individual, the group, the world. Misunderstanding of this artistic science has led to many of the ridiculous notions about magic that still persist today.

WORKING WITH THE FIVE DISCIPLINES

The five fundamentals (concentration, meditation, visualisation, ritual and mediation) correspond to the major symbol of the Circle (as shown in Figure 2) in the following manner:

39

CONCENTRATION	AIR	Origination	BIRTH
MEDITATION	FIRE	Creation	ADULTHOOD
VISUALISATION	WATER	Formation	MATURITY
RITUAL	EARTH	Expression	AGE

The fifth fundamental, that of Mediation, corresponds to the fifth and constant power of Spirit. It may be replaced by the term *Inspiration*, particularly in mystical or religious terminology.

The importance of the three inner disciplines (concentration, visualisation, meditation) is relevant not only to the type of person practising magic, but to the type of training or the school of magical initiation in which the individual is participating. This may be demonstrated by some simple examples.

M is highly imaginative and good at visualising; he is poor on concentration, and his imagination will wander if he is not kept within specific limits by a teacher, an instructional story, or a recording, book or film. He might, in disciplined magical work, choose to build these visual skills for group ritual, in which he becomes a valuable but specifically defined member of joint projects. Alternatively, M could work on exercises to strengthen his weakest area (concentration) and try to achieve an inner balance. This second method is the most difficult, perhaps, but is the one usually taken in traditional and modern magical tuition. The master symbol of the Circle aims at balance, and is not only a map or indicator of the potentials of the human consciousness, but is also used in magical development as an indicator of one's strengths and weaknesses. Thus 'weak' quarters of the Circle are strengthened by a combination of inner disciplines and by ritual work. In magical training creative ritual works as an enabling experience; it unlocks our areas of limitation and re-orders them prior to future growth.

Our second example is F, who is disciplined, efficient and able to concentrate for fairly long periods of time without succumbing to distraction. She enjoys formal pattern-making, in any type of skill, but cannot sit and visualise. She might choose to build her already strong powers of concentration for use in group work, where she would act as a balancing factor or magical but not necessarily sexual or sensual partner for M. Alternatively she might take up training techniques which stimulate her latent inner vision, and so work towards an inner balance.

In both of the above examples, the master symbol of the Circle is used inwardly and outwardly; inwardly as an idealised map (not to be taken literally) of the body-psyche-spirit, and outwardly as a ground plan for the exteriorising of consciousness in ritual. Many of these facets of magical work are dealt with in our other chapters.

CONCENTRATION, VISUALISATION, MEDITATION

These are three *inner* disciplines; they direct consciousness inwards. In advanced stages these three fundamental skills may be directed outwards, but this is impossible for most of us, being a matter of experience rather than discussion or instruction. The normal outward direction of the three inner skills is through ritual pattern making, which is a basic of human consciousness and may be done by anyone without preliminary lengthy training in the inner skills. Indeed, ritual will often unblock latent inner skills in a dynamic manner; but it is not a substitute for the inner skills, as it is a complementary type of action.

There are many books on the three inner skills, and it is not necessary to reproduce here lengthy technical or training material that can be found elsewhere. There are, however, some major differences between eastern and western psychic reactions and methods, and between the general use of meditation or visualisation in magic and in other traditions of altered states of consciousness. Methods of developing concentration are less prone to confusion.

As a general rule, the magician in training should avoid schools of meditation and visualisation that are connected to quasi-religious movements, and certainly of any cult or movement that actively solicits membership and money. A number of relatively pure techniques for concentration and meditation are found in text books (see Bibliography) while visualisation is a faculty that develops rapidly with practice in most cases[5].

Rather than repeat basic instructional material that is dealt with at length in other books, we shall move directly to the most central and significant act of will that precedes all concentration, meditation and visualisation; the will to Silence.

Daily practice at stilling the flow of conditioned awareness, and further stilling or silencing the repetitive inner monologue which we all enact is a guaranteed way into success with the Five Fundamental Arts. Before undertaking any of the inner disciplines, a certain period of time should be spent establishing Silence.

There are a number of methods for this stilling of awareness, and

41

the act of silencing or suspending modes of consciousness reaches deeply to our inherent core of Being. In the beginning, All emerges from Nothing; if we move towards that perfect state of peace from which all Being emerges, our various levels of consciousness/energy are harmonised and realigned.

Silence—Method 1

Sitting comfortably with a straight spine, the magician commences relaxed deep breathing, with eyes closed. The inner Silence is approached by three stages, which gradually still the various activities of consciousness. This technique endures through a whole lifetime, as it is timeless in essence and requires continual development.

The Three Stages

1) The magician stills all his or her *energies,* concentrating on the relaxed breathing pattern, drawing in all energies through the use of the imagination. In other words, we imagine a state in which all energies within and around us are stilled. This act of imagination goes a long way towards an actual stilling of the psychic energies.
2) The magician visualises a dissolution of *space;* all space is reduced to a central core of consciousness; spatial dimensions and concepts cease to exist.
3) Finally, all time is suspended through the active imagination. The magician attempts to enter in to an inner state of *timelessness*.

The order in which the Three Stages are carried out is not important; some workers prefer to commence with a dissolution of Time within their field of consciousness. As Time, Space and Energy are inseparably fused in the nature of the Universe, the threefold dissolution is a relative convenience for human contemplation.

Emerging From Silence

When a state of stillness and silence has been achieved, however briefly, the traditional emergence is made by a deep breathing in and out...one breath that echoes the Breath of Origination, or the drawing in and out of all existence through the power of Being.

After this originative breath, the Worlds and the Circle are visualised or ritually opened. These aspects of magical art are dealt with in our later chapters.

Silence—Method 2

A better known but more complex method is that of withdrawing consciousness from the aspects of existence; this may be done by using the Ten Spheres of the Tree of Life (see Figure 3) combined with rhythmic relaxed breathing. In this method we work from 10 through to 1, withdrawing attention and energy at each stage by meditating briefly on the attributes of the sphere, then dissolving them. Similar methods are widely known through Eastern meditation where consciousness is removed from the various levels of entity by a progressive negation.

Our first method, however (the Three Stages), does not negate the outer realms of entity (such as the body, the mind, the emotion and so on) but causes them to pause and be filled with peace.

Emerging from Silence is carried out as above, though it is possible to utter or imaginatively re-create all Ten Spheres in a pattern of descent of energy from Crown or First Sphere, to Kingdom or the material worlds and the physical body.

Having approached and to a relative extent realised Silence, acts of concentration, visualisation and meditation become increasingly effective. In wisdom traditions of both east and west, a resonant humming chant is often used to attune consciousness to the primal energies such as Silence and emerging Breath. Chants of this sort are the origin of the much-maligned concept of 'words of power'; they act as a super-concentrated key to rapid changes of awareness.

MEDITATION IN MAGIC

Meditation is becoming generally known again in the west, after a lengthy period in which it was confined to monastic religious practices or exercises carried out by the priesthood. We can presume that inner disciplines were rigorously maintained by the magicians or seers of each century, though the techniques of such meditations must be found by interpretation of old legends or poems, or the magical texts, rather than through any specific handbook in its own right. After the commercial influx of pseudo-eastern techniques in the 1960s, there is an increasing awareness and practice of meditation as a genuine discipline, unconnected to cult practices or money-making 'spiritual' organisations. This refining process is very slow, but there is a growing emphasis upon the therapeutic value of meditation which may help to restore the discipline to a more reputable public image.

There are a number of schools or methods of meditation, ranging from commercial ventures (in which money is demanded for technique and instruction or even initiation) to genuine schools or projects or movements, designed to release areas of consciousness seldom used by the average person. The Catholic Church has retained some very specific techniques in the monastic orders and the Society of Jesus; apart from these, most methods found in the west today are offshoots of genuine eastern traditions; some have been adapted badly, others have stood the test of their universality, and endured.

In oral magical training, which comes only from experience and direct tuition rather than from books, there are a number of meditative techniques and exercises which represent the remains of the ancient western system. This system persisted in folk custom in Celtic regions of Britain, and is found fragmented through a number of early texts such as the *Mabinogion*[6] or the *Prophecies* and *Life of Merlin,* or the various mystical Grail texts. But none of these books were designed to teach 'meditation'; they require clarification by an experienced meditator or magician before they can be applied by the student.

Without going into such complex areas as the origins of western meditation and visualisation techniques and imagery, we can illustrate the basics of magical meditation. There are significant differences between general and therapeutic meditation and techniques employed in the magical traditions; with the possible exception of the Church system, mentioned above, it is likely (though not proven) that the methods found within western magical traditions are the remains of a native meditation system, originally connected to the Celtic Druids, the ancient Greeks, and the widespread Mystery cults of the ancient world, many of which persisted in various forms well into the middle ages, surfacing as heretical Christian cults.

To define meditation in the context of ritual magic or visualisation, we must first define the areas in which it is not similar to popular techniques used in the west today, and the fact that it does not have a therapeutic aim.

Magical meditation is not intended as a means of mental or emotional or physical therapy; it may, and often does, have a beneficial effect, but this benefit is derived from any realignment of

44

the flow of consciousness, any relief from the stress of our bizarre culture. The current emphasis upon meditation in therapy may help to make the art more acceptable to the public, but it obscures the deeper aims which have always lain behind such changes of consciousness. In some types of magical meditation, the individual or group may tap into powerful images with healing effects, but this is not a primary aim of magical work.

The magician can and should enter upon a regular programme of meditation, separate from ritual pattern-making. Eventually the interaction between the outer and inner magical disciplines becomes automatic; when ritual and meditation fuse together to gain a higher consciousness, this may lead to *mediation*, which is discussed elsewhere in this book in more detail. Mediation and meditation are two different modes of consciousness, though they are connected in western magical or metaphysical traditions. It is possible and usual to meditate without mediating, but it is unusual, or even inadvisable and unhealthy to attempt to *mediate* without first being skilled in *meditation*.

Traditionally meditation is used to collect and re-focus the awareness towards the core of ritual or ceremony; it is used as a means to an end, and not an end in itself. In magical ceremonies there is a balance between inner and outer action; the outer action is defined by words, movements, physical symbols; the inner action, which is superficially invisible, is established in meditation. In this sense magical meditation is nearer to the controlled consciousness-in-movement that is found in the genuine martial arts, in which inner and outer awareness fuse together to create perfect balance. Conversely, western magical meditation is least like those techniques which rely upon a withdrawal of consciousness from the outer world, including the physical body of the meditator.

There is, however, a deeper level of magical meditation in which a group or individual members, or the single magician, attunes to specific energies, filling the imagination and eventually the total awareness with the energy in question. In this method, a number of meditative techniques are fused together, for it employs the body, the bio-electrical energies, the mind, the emotions, and finally the inward cognition that expands into transpersonal understanding, knowledge, and wisdom. Some of the exercises in this book are designed to work in this manner, and they are modern restatements of well-practised traditional methods. The levels which are merged in magical meditation are as follows:

The Body: ritual movement or position.

Bio-electrical energies: breathing exercises and power centres (though these also work upon other levels).
Mind: recitation and connection of symbols, attributes, other intellectually assimilated connectives in magical art.
Emotions: response to music, colour, inner visions.
Higher consciousness: a fusion of all of the foregoing as a state of *Being.* This may be polarised into formless meditations upon higher orders of awareness such as Understanding, Wisdom, or any of the Paths or transpersonal symbols.

Magical meditation, therefore, re-aligns and inwardly directs consciousness for specific ends; it does not necessarily pass on into *contemplation,* or the higher orders of formless awareness that form the target for mystical and religious devotional practices. This does not imply that these modes of consciousness are not used or are inaccessible, but that in ritual practice, particularly in either early training or in specific advanced operations, they are routed out through the derivative levels (i.e. the lower Spheres upon the Tree of Life or the lower area of the Spindle at the centre of the Wheel of Life).

Before proceeding further, we must examine this difference between formless contemplation and magical meditation further; the individual magician becomes, with practice, skilled in both, but would not route the higher stages through without pre-arranged forms to enable their passage to the outer world. In group work, certain members act as mediators for innerworld images or beings, while others may act in *contemplation* as poles of transcendent awareness which is in turn directed by fellow members using ritual and imagery. At this level of magical work, the group acts as a microcosm, repeating the order of manifestation which is used as a working model for the magical understanding of the universe.

All too often this type of work becomes imbalanced into a state of hierarchy among human officers of the group, but it should be firmly stated that a Circle is round with all stations equidistant from the centre of Being. Our awareness in a state of formless contemplation cannot (usually) radiate this power outward due to the creation-phenomenon known as the Abyss. Conversely, magicians working with highly energised images cannot (usually) connect these to the supernal modes of consciousness within themselves; the situation is one of polarity once again, in this case a bi-polar pattern which runs through all creation. But the bi-polarity does not imply dualism; there are magical ways of by-passing the Abyss which are central to all magical initiation worldwide. Such methods, however, act according to spiritual principles that may not be in accordance with merely human magical endeavour.

In long-term magical programmes of work, handed down through inner and outer traditions, the magician is a creative artist of consciousness rather than a mystical escapologist. Paradoxically, magical traditions do involve physical translation, but not through contemplative withdrawal. In practical terms, these levels of inner discipline are generally inaccessible to the student, but their potential must always be acknowledged.

It should be clear from the foregoing that to work magic we must have some skill and discipline in meditation; but this does not imply a rigid or 'graded' method whereby you must learn to meditate before working ritual. The actual pattern of ritual work at its simplest (and therefore most potent) level, combined with the use of the imagination in visualisation, reaches a long way into magical art. If you can imagine a picture image you can, and already have, become a magician.

MEDIATION

Mediation is the function of a priest or priestess; a mediator is one who intercedes or acts as an interface between Divinity and humanity. In orthodox religion this role is sometimes confused into that of pleading or dictatorial direction, neither of which are functions of a true mediator.

In magic, however, mediation has more precise meaning, based upon the important truth that we all contain Divinity or the original Being within us, just as we are all contained within the Being of the universe. In true mediation, any individual may reach deeply into the states of consciousness where transhuman entities are met. Such beings may be aspects of Divinity, or god-forms, or entities who have transcended human expression and exist solely in the inner worlds. In mediation, a human acts as a focus or gateway for the consciousness of such transhuman beings...but this is not the sole purpose or type of mediation found in magical art.

Just as the transhuman entities (gods, goddesses, masters, saints or in another order archangels and creative spirits) equate with the higher Worlds (see Figures 18 and 19) so do we find reflections of such Worlds and Beings *within ourselves*. In other words, mediation is not a matter of passive reception (as in the popularised and superficial processes of mediumship) but of refining and clarifying personal modes of awareness. When these higher modes are attuned

47

to the Worlds or beings so essential to magical holism mediation may arise.

Most significantly, mediation is not a matter of 'messages'; if it was so, it would be more or less valueless, as higher modes of awareness or higher spiritual energies transcend and obviate verbal communication. A true mediator may be able translate certain key images or intuitions of the spiritual realms into words, but he or she is more likely to act as a channel for a specific power to flow out into the magical circle, or ultimately into the world. It is in this last sense that true priests and priestesses are known; they mediate the power of Divinity.

Thus the initiate working magic, such as the magical rituals or visualisations given in our examples, may become a mediator through the simple act of ritual pattern making and controlled use of the imagination. Just as all humanity partakes of Being, so may we all be priests, priestesses or mediators. The only difference between mediation in magical arts and spiritual inspiration and enlightenment is the technical method employed; the scientific aspect of magic by which proven techniques are taught to successive generations of students, and by which gradual development is made overall through experiment and accumulated knowledge.

In magical art, anyone making a Sign or uttering a Call, or visualising a symbol, is mediating the power of Being through very specific archetypical channels. The more powerful effects of mediation, however, are not usually developed without years of discipline and effort. There is no suggestion here that our inherent spiritual power is likely to result in 'immediate' effects; yet paradoxically this potential is ever present in each and every one of us. Magic is one of the most rapid and dynamic arts for realising our spiritual potential through transformation, interaction and mediation.

4 GROUP RITUAL IN MODERN MAGIC

With the resurgence of interest in magic, there are more people actively engaged in magical arts today than at any period of time during the last thousand years in the west.

Once formal religion collapses or proves fraudulent and unsatis-factory, the collective need for *pattern-making* and the individual quest for truth break out into a variety of expressions. Some of these expressions are chaotic and violent, others are ordered, disciplined and creative. Magical arts, which are innate within our conscious-ness, have a wide variety of practices and practitioners, from the depraved and absurdly gullible to the intelligent and ethical. Many people work magic in groups as a supportive learning process, often on a merely social level, but the art goes far beyond this initial stage and group work has many ramifications that are hardly ever apparent in general or socially-orientated books, courses and public festivals or events.

Most group work is undertaken as experiential work, often with an exploratory aim, with minimal understanding on the part of the participants; this plunging into the unknown is part of the pioneering aspect of the modern revival, but must be taken carefully. There is in fact a vast body of solid technique and knowledge available from tradition, although most of it is ignored by revival magicians, who tend to go for the more glamorous and absurd 'occult' rituals or for very simple social rituals drawn from modern publications. Between these two extremes there are some basic conclusions and methods that can be set out which apply to all workings, preliminary or advanced.

Magical ritual is a system of pattern-making; the patterns act as matrices for energies; the energies are those arising within the consciousness of the ritualists, and can, under specific conditions, involve the bio-electrical energies of the entire complex of body and

49

psyche. The consciousness which merges with and consists of such energies is both individual and collective; it expresses a series of holisms shared by the group within its imagination, including the consensual world or worlds in which the members have their being. This worldview includes not only the outer world of daily life, which is shared in innumerable way by everyone upon the planet, but a very wide range of inner worlds. These inner worlds may be abstractions such as philosophy or religion held in common by the group members, or they may be imaginal dimensions with well-defined inhabitants, landscapes and qualities or functions. Such imaginal worlds are familiar to us all in the stereotypes of 'Heaven and Hell', or the descriptions of fairyland from folklore. In fiction such worlds abound, but these fictional worlds are not identical to the magical inner worlds, which have a real existence independent of the person or persons visualising them.

The holisms within the group imagination derive from a greater consciousness or over-being which is of the fabric of existence. At this stage the theory becomes cosmic rather than human or planetary. Ultimately these various phases are all interwoven; they are selective expressions of one Being, which is being itself.

Lists of devolving correspondences are often found in magical text books; the truth is not as linear or serial as seems apparent in print, for the very nature of the printed page forces a linear or superficially logical progression upon the correspondences. The relationships are spiral or harmonic rather than uni-directional, but for our present purposes of definition a list of connectives in group ritual is summarised as follows:

1) Pattern Making → Ritual → Physical Movements and Location.
2) Matrices → Symbols In Action → Inner Disciplines.
3) Energies → Individual Consciousness → Bio-Electrical Reactions and Shared Consciousness → Group Interactions.
4) Holisms → Shaped Group Consciousness → The World or Worlds.
5) Over-View → Transcendent Awareness → Mediation.

These five aspects of group work do not have hard boundaries; they merge into one another, and will often appear in varying order. A well established example of this harmonic flexibility of order is the occurrence of Mediation or spiritual inspiration, normally assumed to be the culmination of any ritual. Flashes of transcendent consciousness often occur, however, at the very opening of a magical ritual, before preliminary pattern-making, at the moment of crossing

50

TITLE	SCENE	HOUR	ORGAN	ART	COLOUR	SYMBOL	TECHNIC
1. Telemachus	The Tower	8 a.m.		Theology	White, Gold	Heir	Narrative
2. Nestor	The School	10 a.m.		History	Brown	Horse	Catechism (pe...
3. Proteus	The Strand	11 a.m.		Philology	Green	Tide	Monologue (male)
4. Calypso	The House	8 a.m.	Kidney	Economics	Orange	Nymph	Narrative (mature)
5. Lotus-eaters	The Bath	10 a.m.	Genitals	Botany, Chemistry		Eucharist	Narcissism
6. Hades	The Graveyard	11 a.m.	Heart	Religion	White, Black	Caretaker	Incubism
7. Aeolus	The Newspaper	12 noon	Lungs	Rhetoric	Red	Editor	Enthymemic
8. Lestrygonians	The Lunch	1 p.m.	Esophagus	Architecture		Constables	Peristaltic
9. Scylla and Charybdis	The Library	2 p.m.	Brain	Literature		Stratford, London	Dialectic
10. Wandering Rocks	The Streets	3 p.m.	Blood	Mechanics		Citizens	Labyrinth
11. Sirens	The Concert Room	4 p.m.	Ear	Music		Barmaids	*Fuga per canonem*
12. Cyclops	The Tavern	5 p.m.	Muscle	Politics		Fenian	Gigantism
13. Nausicaa	The Rocks	8 p.m.	Eye, Nose	Painting	Grey, Blue	Virgin	Tumescence, detumescence
14. Oxen of the Sun	The Hospital	10 p.m.	Womb	Medicine	White	Mothers	Embryonic development
15. Circe	The Brothel	12 midnight	Locomotor Apparatus	Magic		Whore	Hallucination
16. Eumaeus	The Shelter	1 a.m.	Nerves	Navigation		Sailors	Narrative (old)
17. Ithaca	The House	2 a.m.	Skeleton	Science		Comets	Catechism (impersonal)
18. Penelope	The Bed		Flesh			Earth	Monol...

Source: Stuart Gilbert, *James Joyce's Ulysses*, p. 38 (Penguin Books, Harmondsworth, 1963)

game of literary *Cluedo*. Scholars went to great lengths to establish that Leopold Bloom moved along a north-westerly axis through Dublin, just as Odysseus did through the Mediterranean. None of this had been part of Stuart Gilbert's intention. He, in 1930, had good reasons for emphasizing the deliberated symmetries of a book which, by then, had won for Joyce the dubious reputation -of a heedless improviser or autistic surrealist. But Gilbert's very success robbed later readers of a certain innocence. Thereafter, the hilarious moment in Barney Kiernan's pub, when Bloom shakes a cigar at the chauvinist citizen, would be incomplete without the additional knowledge that this is a parody of the Homeric scene in which Odysseus launches a burning stake of olive wood and blinds the Cyclops. To elaborate further details of such a parallel is often possible and sometimes helpful – as may be seen in many books of annotations – but there is always the danger that a tracing of the Homeric structure usurps the experience of reading the text. A later critic, High Kenner, insisted that the object in reading a book is not to reconstruct the *schema*, just as the aim in eating a dinner is not to reconstitute the recipe. Nonetheless, many fine dinner parties have afforded guests the extra pleasure of guessing the mystery ingredients of a praised dish, and have ended with pleas for a copy of the formula to take away.

In the course of *Ulysses*, Joyce was frequently at pains to advertise his formula. The text abounds in ironic self-references. In the National Library scene, the Quaker librarian reports the portentous opinions of one Dr Sigerson with wide-eyed innocence: 'Our national epic has yet to be written ... Moore is the man for it.' Good idea, wrong writer, laughs the

the threshold from outer to inner awareness. This pre-event occurs because transcendent or spiritual consciousness (which is mediated at the culmination of a rite) is not bound by our serial relationship to time. During such pre-events, we have 'jumped time' to the deepest aspect of the pattern of the ritual. This does not imply that we should stop ritual work if such a pre-event occurs, nor that we should aim for the transcendent leap without the analogous pattern (as is done in mysticism). In magic, higher consciousness is brought through into the time-bound world in a highly-concentrated form, and channelled through mediating patterns towards its goal. Magic aims ultimately to change the world, hence the popular notion of miraculous or quite paradoxical results obtainable from ritual work. Such results manifest firstly within the magician, not in the illusory world of material aims and misdirections.

The entire question of *manifestation* brings us to the second phase of group work, which is in many ways a reversal or recapitulation of the first five stages, though it need not pass through all five to be effective, and may leap over any or all stages under powerful magical direction. The first phase (outlined above) defines the inward-reaching acts of magic, with *Mediation* as the hinge or turning point. The second phase (outlined below) defines the outward-reaching acts of magic, through which the mediation or power flows.

6) Mediation of greater consciousness brings transformative power.

7) Holisms or group images are vitalised and changed by this power.

8) Energies flow through the group images into the individual consciousness and organisms of the members of the group.

9) The physical, biological and psychic reactions are channelled by the matrices established through inner disciplines (concentration, visualisation and meditation) and by the pattern-making and symbols of the ritual itself.

10) The energies finally manifest in the physical world through the manipulation of symbols (such as glyphs, images, magical objects or implements, patterns of movement) but effectively through the human and environmental relationship, through changes in the shared 'reality' or worldview, the so-called 'real' world.

BALANCE IN GROUP WORK

A typical magical group may have twelve members, or as few as three. Two workers usually enact *polarity magic*, and as such do not

WHEEL OF LIFE

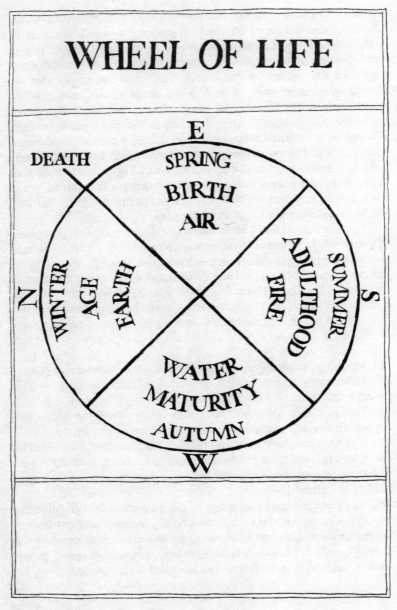

Figure 2.   *The Wheel of Life (I).*

constitute a group, though within the group pairs and triads of workers will cause quite complex polarity patterns to be generated.

When groups reach larger sizes, traditionally that of thirteen members, they tend to break up. During the centuries of persecution, this cellular system was used deliberately much as it is today in political groups. But it derives from an organic factor, in which survival and dissemination occurs through separation. This natural law of growth and interaction explains the dreary, much-publicised and juvenile disputes among the magicians of the early part of the twentieth century. The break up of magical groups is not a matter of destructive power, as in the nuclear reaction of fission upon reaching critical mass, but of the spiral and re-iteration shown by the Wheel of Life (see Figure 2).

A typical group might have eight members, with four acting as officers of the Quarters (East, South, West, North) and four at the cross-Quarters (South-East, South-West, North-West, North-East). To this combination, an unlimited number of other members may be added in various typical patterns. Large organisations become disruptive and difficult due to our human weaknesses. The hierarchical tendencies of some magical orders are merely obscure examples of human greed for power; in the true magical circle all members are equal and balance one another. There are no 'masters' or starring roles in properly formulated ritual. This viewpoint is contrary to many of the magical practices taught in the literary schools of 'occultism', in which high grades and personality inflation often seem more important than any genuine creative magic. One of the features of modern magical arts is the return to an equal and open magical system, with no physical hierophant or leader, but a truly magical and inner direction mediated by all members around the Circle.

In practical work, each individual has certain strong abilities and certain weaknesses; the circular pattern with its derivative squares and triangles is used to create an overall balance. This balance helps to mould a powerful group imagination in which the psychic totality holds all the required qualities and skills collectively, yet is able to act during the rite as one entity. The more skilful the members, the more effective this group entity will be. Magical arts have always recognised individuality within a communal higher order, which eventually becomes individuality upon transcendent levels of consciousness.

Physical gender is not necessarily the guide to magical roles or the functions of any specific person within the group. As a general rule the officers of the Quarters are often defined sexually, but on inner levels this stereotyping is soon reduced to nonsense.

SEXUAL DEFINITION OF THE MAGICAL CIRCLE

EAST: MALE. Element of Air; implement of Sword or Arrow.
SOUTH: MALE. Element of Fire; implement of Staff or Rod.
WEST: FEMALE. Element of Water; implement of Vessel or Cup.
NORTH: FEMALE. Element of Earth; implement of Mirror or Shield.

The combined group entity is thus androgynous, partaking equally of male and female qualities. This mysterious para-human consciousness is described in the myths which relate that the original human was physically bisexual, or that male and female were physically joined as a dual entity or androgyne. This latent androgyny is physically or biologically present in every male and female; furthermore, on inner levels of consciousness, we change sexual role repeatedly. This has been commented upon and labelled by modern psychology, but magical arts take the polarities much further. The theme of roles and inner and outer polarity will be found running through this book, as it runs through all magical interactions.

To work a magical ritual, group members balance one another on impersonal inner levels. They may also interact personally, as married couples, lovers or friends. In magic, personal interactions are generally set aside for higher aims, and one of the hardest lessons is not to confuse magical relationships with expressed sexual relationships. This same phenomenon is known in a slightly different form to medical practitioners or psychologists, where the patient (a passive role) reacts sexually and emotionally to the therapist (an active role).

As a general rule, members of magical groups are friendly towards one another, but in advanced workings it is possible for individuals who would not normally interact to work together for a specific project.

The subject of polarity, so essential to group ritual work, is not limited to the collection of humans in the outer worlds. It runs through all existence without exception, and wisdom traditions are deeply concerned with teaching and experience of polarity.

The symbols found in many of our diagrams are archetypes of creation, but they are also circuits of polarity or cycles of energy. The most sophisticated and accessible of these is the glyph known as the Tree of Life, which demonstrates polar relationship between the origin of Being and the expressed material worlds through Ten Spheres or relative modes of power, connected by twenty-two Paths, or fusions between the power of the Spheres. The Paths are

54

sometimes regarded as channels through which the energies of each Sphere flow, but this forces us into a linear conception of the Tree of Life which deprives it of much of its magical effect upon human consciousness.

The Tree acts for both the Macrocosm or universe and the Microcosm or human entity. Thus it shows not only cosmic manifestation, but the fusion of energies within a human entity; it also gives remarkable insight into the polarisations of interaction, either between humans or humans and other forms of consciousness/energy.

Having summarised many of the basic aspects of magical art, we now progress to ten chapters which are derived from each of the Ten Spheres. These are not lists of attributes, but reflections upon the qualities or powers of each sphere as they apply to modern magical art in human society.

5 THE TREE OF LIFE

I have not adhered to a rigid development of the Tree of Life in the following chapters, as this has been done repeatedly by so many authors, ranging from absurdly complex treatises to simplistic summaries or mere lists, that yet another book of attributes would be valueless or even tedious. Useful books summarising the Tree of Life are listed in the bibliography, but a few words about its general role in modern magical art may be helpful.

The Tree is a pan-cultural symbol used in mysticism, meditation and magical arts in the west. Although modern literature is most familiar with the mathematical Hebrew/Arabic variant, which percolated through Europe during the Renaissance, magical Tree symbolism is inherent in western culture and the Tree was employed as a visionary and educational symbol long before the influx of Hebrew mysticism which continues to confuse modern literary occultists. Furthermore, the use of the Tree in western traditions of transforming consciousness is still changing; the rigid western Kabbalist uses systems which are often far removed from genuine Hebrew mysticism, while the less rigid simpler systems which are gradually appearing in general use are, in some ways, a reversion to the older more direct form of the Tree prior to the many intellectual accumulations found in literature.

The Tree is a symbol of connection; it shows relationships, connective patterns, nothing more. The patterns may be related in our imagination to the creation of the Universe, or to the energy cycles of the human being; the Tree of Life acts as an indicator, a map, upon which the changes of reality which occur in magic may be loosely defined.

In the following pages I have avoided the use of anglicised Hebrew terms, as these seem quite preposterous in a western context where

56

the language is not spoken. The various Spheres and Paths of the Tree, which are shown in the diagrams, are referred to in simple descriptive terms without any aura of pseudo-secrecy or intellectual mystique, these being the two great weakening trends in occultism. In so doing, I am not suggesting that genuine Hebrew scholars with mystical intent, working within their own culture, should change one fraction of their hallowed traditions; merely that such traditions have their equivalent in the west, which may be redefined during the current renaissance of magical arts.[7]

The Tree belongs properly to oral tradition ('Kabbalah' means literally an oral, mouth-to-ear, tradition of wisdom), and the reasons for this are clear if we consider native magical origins. A tree has its roots in the earth, it reaches through the world of nature with its cycle of the seasons, but its crown is in the sky; thus it lives in several worlds at once: under-earth, earth, over-earth, sky. The cosmic or universal Tree extends from the stars to the formless depths of space, just as an earthly tree grows from the land towards the sun. Upon its branches symbols are hung; creatures live in and on the green shady leaves and twigs, while creatures of a quite different sort live in the hollows of its roots. To our ancestors, trees were magical beings, not in a superficially intellectual manner of correspondences, but as living powerful creatures who permeated the worlds, and who reflected the Being that permeates all worlds.

In using the Tree extensively in this book, I am following well-established educational traditions; to assemble magical material according the traditional patterns in which it was once taught is essential, even when writing a book. But I do not repeat basic texts on Kabbalah, and often move away from the rigid numerical development of the Tree, which normally runs from Sphere One in the origins of Being to Sphere Ten in the manifested world or worlds. In using the Tree in this expansive manner, I am confident that I follow the root magical traditions of the west, in which the fruit of magical encounter is more valuable by far than pages of wordy theory.

To those who have knowledge of westernised Kabbalah, I humbly plead for patience in dealing with this reassessment; and to those who encounter the Tree of Life for the first time in these pages and pictures, I would say that it poses a map not for the greatest adventure of them all, but for the only adventure that has any true reality, the adventure from which all other events devolve; the path of living consciousness across and within the cycle of the universe and its countless worlds.

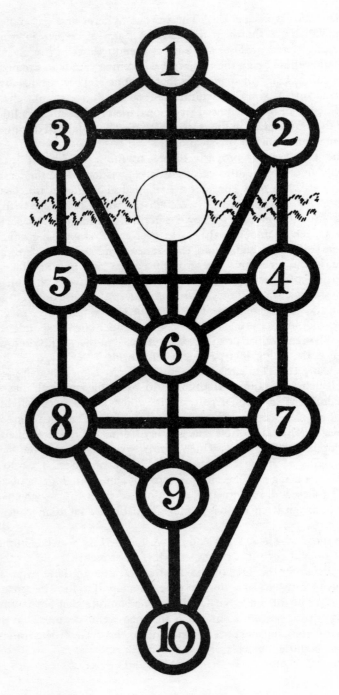

Figure 3.   The Tree of Life.

1) Original Source of Being out of Non-Being. The first breath of the universe, the seed of consciousness and energy. This Sphere is Neutral, balanced, or pre-polarisation. The CROWN of the Tree of Life.
2) WISDOM: primal power in motion. Associated with active analytic 'male' divine energy. The utterance of the Word or Worlds.
3) UNDERSTANDING: primal vessel that contains power. Associated with catalytic receptive 'female' divine energy. The Great Mother.
4) MERCY (The Giver): a reflection or harmonic of (2) in which the energies of creation issue across the Abyss. The positive anabolic male power of giving-out. This power works upon a cosmic level; it is the building force of creation.
5) SEVERITY (The Taker): harmonic vessel of (3). Catabolic, receptive, female. Represented in traditions worldwide by a severe female divinity often of fierce aspect. The cosmic destroying force, breaking down and purifying. Frequently ascribed to a male god-form (Mars) in relatively modern literature, due to misunderstanding of the polarity of the Tree pattern.
6) CENTRALITY or BEAUTY or HARMONY: balanced fusion of all energies. A hermaphrodite or bi-sexual power which reflects the Crown and acts as the central focus for all energies below the Abyss which separates the upper Triad (1/2/3) from the remainder of the Tree. Traditionally this is the realm of the Saviour, the Sons of Light, the Divine Kings. It also represents the Sun of our solar system.
7) VICTORY: the Young Goddess or Flower Maiden. The emotions. An anabolic active female sphere. Associated with Venus traditionally.
8) HONOUR: the young god. The intellect. A catabolic receptive male power. Both Honour and Victory exchange polarities. Associated with Hermes.
9) FOUNDATION: male and female united. The matrix of expressed life forms and materialised energy; all previous Spheres fuse together. Associated with the Moon goddesses and gods.
10) KINGDOM: the expressed world drawn from all of the foregoing. Paradoxically this world is closest to the CROWN.

THREE PILLARS DEFINED

There are Three Pillars or polarisations overall; left, right, centre. The Central Pillar (which is the spindle of the sphere of the universe) is neutral, bi-sexual or balanced. The left-hand Pillar is feminine and catalytic, while the right-hand is masculine and analytic. There is an overall rotation from bottom centre (10) through 8/5/3/1 and returning 1/2/4/7 to 10. This cycle turns upon the pivot of 6.

A second rotation is found between left and right (2–3/4–5/7–8) while a third rotation is found between the Crown and the Kingdom or Being and Matter. These three conceptual rotations lock together to form the overall Sphere of Being.

The divisions and rotations are immensely valuable subjects for meditation upon polarity and harmonic phases of reality in truth. The fusion and interaction of the Spheres forms the connections known as Paths; these are defined in our chapter on the Tarot Trumps.

MAGICAL SYSTEMS

There are two ways of looking at magical systems such as the Tree of Life, the Circle, the worlds of manifestation, and similar patterns that are learned by the student. Firstly they may be seen as rigid lists, and this encyclopedic view seems supported by the medieval obsession with comprehensive lists and correspondences, an attitude which also seems to persist well into modern magical literature. But such lists appear during transitions from oral tuition to the written or printed word; in so doing they lose much of their magical value as incantations in which the length, rhythm and sonority are as important, or possibly more important, than the details.

Due to a strong tendency towards rigidity in western cultural development, the magical lists, once taught by word of mouth and recited under heightened circumstances of awareness, have become authoritarian, invested with a formal almost legal value that may be quite alien to their magical origins.

The second way of looking at the lists, as implied above, is to see them as aids to development, and nothing more. They have the same role in magic as exercises have in music for beginners; although repetitive and even boring, they enable us to accumulate a totality of skill that comes from a deep conditioning in which the body, mind and emotions fuse together as one. In the musician it is expressed as talent disciplined through performance, in the magician it is expressed as actual operation of magic in which practical work replaces all theory.

It must be stressed that the student should not become obsessed with systems, and that in advanced stages the systems are disposed of utterly, and replaced by higher orders of energy. A competent magician can apply his or her ability to almost any magical system, but this rare competence is only obtained by strict adherence to specific teaching traditions, and cannot be found through hopping or window-shopping from system to system, tradition to tradition.

When experienced workers with transformed perceptions meet, they are able to communicate regardless of their cultural origins; in their own way, through their own traditional systems, each has transcended the limitations of awareness that define cultural differences. It is likely that each of our two theoretical masters began early training with extensive lists, never forgotten, but seldom applied in maturity.

6 ORIGINATION

What is the origin of the magical arts? This typically modern question would have been meaningless to our ancestors; for them 'magic' was an integral part of their life pattern. Today we feel obliged to analyse such matters, as if by labelling or knowing their origins we can actually claim to understand or even grow beyond them. One of the most important functions of magic has always been asking the right questions, a theme found repeatedly in myth and legend, and epitomised in the west by the mystical quest for the Grail. The answers to questions about the origin of magic are not, perhaps, as obvious as we might assume.

There are a number of well-published theories dealing with origins of magic in the supposedly primitive past; most of these theories revolve around the concept of 'sympathy' in which primitives built their magical techniques and philosophy directly from the need to survive and control the hunt or the herd, or in later cultures the crop. Behaviour linked to the means of survival is said to have had a *sympathetic* effect upon the material worlds; a drawing of a dead deer would lead to a good hunt; a mime of sexual activity (or real sexual activity) would bring fruitful fields and herds. Theories of this type were very popular during the Victorian period and in the early years of the twentieth century; a great deal of modern psychology derives directly from such concepts, even today. In anthropology and comparative religion the theory of sympathetic magic played a very influential role; magic was explained and labelled by a rational and potentially historical model, often drawing upon contemporary primitive cultures by way of comparison.

Modern studies of folklore and anthropology, psychological experiments, and the rapid advance of actual magical practice on an experiential level rather than mere theory, have proved the concept of *sympathy* to be far too simplistic. Magical arts worldwide and

61

through time share certain harmonic characteristics which simply will not be explained away by a condescending rational formula. The formula still appears in print frequently, and acts as an unacknowledged foundation for many otherwise perceptive books and studies. But we cannot subscribe today to the worldview that generated the historical theory of magic building up slowly from the crude notions of primitives; we no longer accept the originally self-evident superiority of the white rational (usually male) mentality, to which all other races were lesser intellects bound in the darkness of superstition. This remarkable assumption was extended to our own ancestors, and is found in many historical theories and pictures of early cultures which have repeatedly been shown to be false by archaeology and other advancing researches into the past. The traditions of so-called primitive people, including our own not-too-distant ancestors, are now proving to be more complex and subtle, more effective as carriers of a deep transpersonal wisdom, than could ever have been dreamed of by the theorists of the last century.

We shall not, therefore, follow the same old introduction to the living magical arts that may be found in numerous other books, partly historical, partly psychological, and utterly limited by the pseudo-rational urge to 'explain' everything away and reduce it to a mere quirk of human behaviour. Such an approach to magic is truly more ignorant than the ignorance presumed upon our ancestors by the theory of 'sympathetic magic'. We shall approach the subject from a quite different direction, hopefully sidestepping many dull and fruitless areas of correspondence and comparison . . . areas that are really fictitious.

If we look for a new definition of magical art, we will not find one; long long ago the ancient Mysteries defined the beginning and end of all magic, be it white, black, muddy or rainbow-coloured; it was 'Mankind, know thyself'.

Superficially this may seem to be a very materialist rational injunction; but the ancients were well aware that the self, or inner knowledge, was a mirror or harmony of a profound awareness. By looking within we pierce the veils that surround our limitations and approach the mysteries of understanding creation. Nor is this a wildly poetical statement; it conforms to the aims of science, physics, art or music, in which an intuition or deduction is made inwardly and then resolved and manifested as an outward form. In this sense all human activity is truly magical.

Magical traditions, however, are very specific; they have powerful and often surprising effects when they are correctly applied. In the later chapters of this book, we will encounter some of the most

62

effective methods of such application, which are open to individual experiment and confirmation. The type of magic concerned does not derive from sympathetic magic although this does form a superficial part of the worldview of certain cultures. It comes from a deeper level altogether, in which modes of *self-knowledge* are paramount. In other words, men and women grasped the curious intuitions, concepts and dreams, exteriorised their meditations, and formally applied such qualities or modes of consciousness. They exteriorised their *imagination*, not merely for obvious material ends, but from deep levels in which consciousness apprehended the mysteries of the universe. Why else would early cultures have generated such profound knowledge of stellar patterns, a knowledge which could have no rational relationship to the crudities of sympathetic magic? Modern researchers are still finding the remarkable accuracy and endurance of such lore, yet it developed and in some cases still exists, in cultures which are repeatedly labelled as 'primitive' or 'ignorant'. And this is merely one of the aspects of living magical art.

Exteriorising the imagination, giving form to intuitions, is quite different from the concept of ignorance building up chains of connection until a magical system is established. The first model draws from primal or archetypical symbols shared by humankind despite varieties of expression, while the second merely devolves from custom and practice, presumed needs and desires.

ORIGINS OF MAGICAL ART AND ORIGINS OF THE UNIVERSE

To put the origins of magic in more mystical or poetic terms, we could say that, just as Being was breathed forth from Non-Being, so do we as human reflections of divinity have a mysterious spiritual power within us. Physically this is represented by our breath, our life energy, but metaphysically it is the seed of our very existence. Magic originated as a response to the spiritual impulse; with time it developed as an artistic science designed (and proven by repeated experiments) to reattune our awareness to the inner spirit.

The most potent aspects of magic are the simplest, for they reiterate the essential simplicity of origination. All magical patterns and behaviour derive not from conditioned response but from inner impulses that hold within themselves the archetypical patterns of all Being.

7 THE POWER THAT ENABLES MAGIC

In the popular and prejudiced misconceptions regarding magic, a great deal of nonsense is talked about mysterious powers and how these powers are employed by the magician. It is as if such so-called powers run contrary to the normal, powerless, human situation; they are presumed to be undesirable or possibly if not actually evil and corrupt. Yet such volumes of lurid protestation show where the desire truly lives; those who shout the loudest about unhallowed powers and evil are exactly those most susceptible to such fantastical temptations.

The effect of magic is proven by experience rather than through dogma or shrill argument; the patterns of both theory and practice in magical arts are well established, and it is possible to make a number of statements regarding magical work and the enabling power from which it derives.

In later chapters, we shall examine the expression of magical energies through the human being, the natural world, the body, the psyche, and the four Elements. But these are the *expressive* levels of magical philosophy; before such levels are reached, there are formative and creative levels of energy, which include the imagination and a pattern of consciousness attuned to an originative level at which Being emerges from Non-Being. These metaphysical realms occupied our ancestors' attention for many centuries; the entire area of speculation manifests today as stellar and nuclear physics.

The building of a conceptual model of magical philosophy has always been one of the basic aims of the Mysteries, of magical and mystical schools or systems. Various models or maps available to us today vary in their vocabulary and their cultural origins, but not in the primal patterns of understanding that they express. Such patterns are inherent, though immensely flexible, within human consciousness; they arise from intuition and imagination filtered through the emotions and intellect; they express our relationship to elemental, planetary and stellar cycles. Magic is a practical art or craft which re-applies the intellectual and emotional vocabularies to the primal energies found within the intuition and the imagination.

There is only one enabling Power behind all magic, mysticism or religious impulse; the Power of Being. Anything that *is*, which is to say everything in or out of relative states of defined existence, holds within it the Power of Being. In magic, as in modern physics, the expressed form is merely a field or mask or mode for inherent energy. Magical traditions teach the relative states or worlds apprehended through human consciousness, particularly in altered states of awareness that transcend or underpin habitual directions of attention.

In orthodox religions worldwide, the Being is called a god or goddess; in mysticism it is perceived as a wholeness, from which parts devolve or derive without ever losing the identity of the original whole. In modern science it is defined as formulae relating matter and energy, but consciousness is excluded from this worldview.

In magical arts, all existence, no matter what the form, has consciousness. This is not an idle superstition hanging over from primitive ignorant cultures, but the key to a profound relationship between the human psyche and the universe.

We should not be deceived into presuming that the consciousness implied is similar to our own habitual patterns, especially as we know so little about ourselves. Some of the superficially strange positions taken by magical psychology are designed to radically alter our self-image, even the collective self-image of the so-called 'human condition'.

There is a curious danger in the standard anthropological or sympathetic-magic theory often wheeled out to explain the origins of esoteric philosophy or practical ritual; it is assumed that people who claim to find consciousness in stones or trees inevitably define it as a humanised anthropomorphic awareness. Even in modern psychology we are repeatedly taught that myths are based upon personifications of the powers of nature, as well as the patterns inherent in the human psyche. While this is undeniably true in part, it is by no means the whole picture or an adequate explanation.

Magicians, modern or primitive, seek to relate to the consciousness in matter of natural forms such as trees, stones, springs or wells, not because they see such entities as having human-like responses, but because the interaction between such beings and the human magician creates a path or holism within a greater consciousness which is shared by both. This is the scientific aspect of magical practice which is so often derided or overlooked; it is a science of intuition and imagination combined with well-established theory and practical methods.

The power that enables magic is that same power or energy that enables the nuclear reaction, generates stars and galaxies, causes the Universe and its life forms to come into being. At such a universal level, the image is incomprehensible, no mere human can imagine or propose to handle such powers...or can they? We have dared in physics to do exactly what has long been foreseen and proposed in magic, to directly harness the powers of creation and destruction inherent in the universe of Being. The major difference is that the magician, primitive or sophisticated, knows that all the multiplicity of forms have *consciousness*, but the physicist states that all forms have interconnected *energies*. In the human being, consciousness and energy are undeniably fused together; we are not able to separate the two by materialist science any more than we may do so through magical arts.

To assist our understanding of the power of Being and its paths of expression, magical teaching traditions have generated maps or models or symbol structures which encapsulate and also transcend lengthy verbal or written descriptions. The illustrations in this book are merely modern re-statements of those traditional teaching aids; they should be examined carefully in connection with the relevant text of each chapter. One of the curious properties of such symbols is that we do not outgrow them; there are no 'beginners' symbols in magic, the basic set remains the same for all levels of work, from the student to the advanced magical adept. During development, and with growing ability to work with higher or more potent modes of power, some of the attributes of the symbols will vary; certain sub-patterns are used for special projects or purposes, but the basic maps, glyphs and symbols remain constant.

This property is fascinating, and is never given sufficient attention in formal books or studies of magical arts. Far from the most powerful symbol or ritual being the most obscure and complicated (as is frequently presumed in popular notions about so-called occultism) the most simple units are the most effective. They remain with the magician for a lifetime, or for many lifetimes, and are harmonics of the power of Being inherent throughout the universe.

The enabling power of magic is not derived from absurd bargains or contracts with forbidden or demonic beings, but from a living set of symbols that act as interfaces or matrices between the human being and the universal Being. Such glyphs or maps as are found in magical tuition act as areas of focus for the human consciousness, but they also harmonise with many other types of consciousness in many worlds.

Put more simply, a power runs throughout existence; it has endless expressions, circuits, rotations, cycles or paths. But these expressions are merely fragments or reflections of greater inclusive patterns that appear in the consciousness of the magicians as a series of key images. The deliberate use of such images or symbols links together forms or paths of energy (consciousness) which are normally presumed to be separate, or even non-existent. By such means magical traditions may teach methods to see the future or the past, the abilities to apprehend events from a distance, or the activation of the therapeutic energies with the body-psychic complex or bio-electrical energy field. They also teach regarding the relationship between human and other types of being; this is an essential part of magical work, which we shall return to in detail in later chapters.

We must not think that symbols such as those found in the illustrations merely 'represent' modes of consciousness, as if the symbol was in some way a lesser substitute for the real thing. If symbols are approached in this manner, they either do not work fully or fail to operate at all. In magical practice, as in magical psychology, the symbol and the power are interchangeable; in fact the symbol *is* the power.

This may be a difficult concept for many people, even for certain practising magicians who treat symbols as dramatic props rather than as living entities of conscious energy. The truth of this matter can only be found in meditation rather than in explanation, yet some initial grounding in the relationship between symbols and power or energies is required before genuine magical work can be undertaken.

In material work of any sort, such as the construction of an artifact, the object to be built is first defined by symbols such as its plan, description or formula. Such apparently obvious methods of work reflect those used in magical art and defined in metaphysics, where archetypes act as moulds or matrices for the expression of energy into a defined form. But this analogy does not apply fully to magical symbols, for they are not mere plans or measurements for a single job of work; neither are cosmic archetypes such plans.

A magical symbol, such as the Wheel of Exchange, the Fourfold Pattern, or the Tree of Life, is the nearest expression within human awareness of the true function of an archetype or set of related archetypes; they are the maps or matrices by which Being expresses itself in an immense holistically-related variety of energetic forms.

If we look for an enabling power that makes magic in our human world, we must grasp not only the mystical intuition that such power is inherent in all Being, but we must also attune our individual consciousness to symbols that act as gates or matrices for that Being. Such symbols may even be divorced from physical concepts of reality, while remaining true to artistic or mystical reality. Ultimately it is the imagination that transforms the physical collective or habitual world.

Magical symbols, therefore, are living entities of power in a mode or pattern; they cannot be outgrown or passed over; there are no secrets in magic, no advanced symbols retained for the elite. Anyone who works patiently with a small number of primal symbols may unlock all doors to all worlds; the symbols are the keys to a constantly transforming and maturing consciousness.

In traditional invocations, god-names are employed. In the western religions, the god-name is drawn from Hebrew culture, and is known as Jehovah or YHVH (Yahweh). What does this actually mean?

In magical terms it is a human way of expressing that cosmic emergence or explosion of power which generates the stars within the dark of space. The vessel is of course the Great Mother. Magic is frequently concerned with alphabets, and the power of letters and words in western magical arts has unfortunately been confused by the use of Hebrew mystical vocabulary taken out of cultural context. The old western alphabet of magic, if we accept the arguments put forward by the late Robert Graves[8], is likely to have been defined by trees rather than by letters alone, but in all primal cultures the entire scope of nature is a living language that tells of divinity, of cycles, of power and of regeneration.

The power that enables magic is that great mysterious power that originates the universe, shown as the second Sphere of the Tree of Life; but it is also the echo of the Word within ourselves. When the two reflections are joined as one, the entire universe is complete.

8 UNDERSTANDING MAGICAL TRADITIONS AND TECHNIQUES

Tradition and technique have been placed together in this chapter intentionally. There are no magical techniques divorced from traditions; in many branches of the art the tradition *is* the technique. The nature of magic is such that, although the basics may be isolated to a certain extent for general explanation, a true understanding of the art is only gained by personal involvement in a living tradition. Just as no man is an island, no magician may practise technique in intellectual isolation. Paradoxically, this emphatically does not mean that the student or advanced worker is obliged to join groups, orders or societies; the union with a tradition, which is a coherent collective stream of consciousness, is found within rather than without.

Symbols, energy, techniques and traditions are all harmonically related; the relationship is found through meditation and ritual work. Just as power manifests through symbols, so does tradition manifest through technique; the first mode, power or tradition, is given a localised temporal outlet through the second mode, symbol or technique. On inner levels, this separation dissolves.

One of the weaknesses of modern occultism is the literary emphasis upon superficial technique; the right words, the right images, the correct authority, the proper way to extinguish a candle; such details are given quite spurious weight without recourse to the traditions in which they may have originated. Much of this nonsense is cut through cleanly by a simple magical law: *seek to understand the tradition, and the techniques will regenerate within your imagination.*

Lack of living tradition is a problem which has been partly resolved through a revival of paganism, and an increased general awareness of the relationship between humankind and nature; magic is no longer practised solely by intellectuals locked into city centre lodges, brandishing their candles and mumbling badly-pronounced Hebrew. Increasing research and publication during the twentieth century has slowly built up substantial evidence of western esoteric traditions, which were never lost or destroyed, but overlooked and ignored for several generations by all but a small minority.

To work effective magic, we need not only to understand the power of tradition generally, but to identify separate branches. There are a number of major traditions which interconnect, and many sub-traditions that rise and fall from the bubbling cauldron of collective symbolic stock. Sub-traditions are particularly interesting to the magical adept, as they may be employed for specific purposes much as an artist may use a studio set up and hired for only one or a limited number of commissions. Some are aligned to ancient sites, others are the results of careful work by magicians of previous generations while others derive entirely from inner worlds hardly contacted by humanity. In order, however, to employ sub-traditions or sub-systems in this manner, one needs to understand the major traditions from which they are derived.

A short survey of western traditions and their relationship with one another is valuable to the magician; the analysis which follows is not based upon the standard historical-literary viewpoint found in general publication, but upon the inner or harmonic connections between the traditions. All traditions defined here, however, rely upon the basic symbols or close variants indicated in our illustrations; such primal keys are known worldwide, but the uniquely eastern or western qualities of a tradition derive from the relationship between the environment, the land, and the people developing in that land through the ages.

Figure 4 shows the relationship between the western traditions and their foundation in a chthonic source that still underpins all magical work, though it is seldom employed in its own right by modern magicians due to ignorance of its existence; the magical realm of the Underworld[9].

PAGANISM

Due to state or political religious propaganda of previous centuries, the term pagan still has suggestions of evil or barbarism or ignorance to many people. If we seriously consider classical or native pagan evidence in Europe, this scurrilous picture is rapidly disproven. But in the last twenty years (1960–1980 onwards) the word *pagan* has developed a new meaning in the popular press, or perhaps it is a return to its original meaning; a pagan is one who practises a pre-Christian form of worship. Paganism must be separated from

70

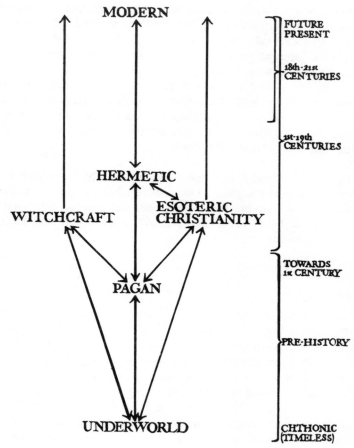

Figure 4. Emergence of Traditions. Note: this chart does not correspond to a Tree of Life.

TRADITIONS	TECHNIQUES
Paganism	Drawn from ancient religions and magical schools.
Witchcraft	Drawn from remains of a specific nature cult.
Hermetic	Intellectual fusion of pagan gnostic and esoteric Christian practices and philosophies.
Modern occultism	Merges Hermetic and psychological theories.
Esoteric Christian	Drawn from heretical and mystical traditions banned by the orthodox churches.

71

witchcraft for it may incorporate a very large number of complex sources ranging from native Celtic gods and goddesses through to classical Greek; it may also form contacts with earlier cultures such as Egypt or ancient Atlantis. Each of these cultural traditions is pagan; they often arise in magical visualisation and tuition, for the experience of our forebears is ever present for us to learn from. In certain specific magical techniques, Hermetic methods, pagan traditions are merged with esoteric Christian material; this fusion is the true cultural picture of the relationship between Christianity and its ancestors rather than false confrontation and elitist or ignorant conflict.

The fusion is found to a certain extent in the orthodox churches of each country, where saints and other revered images are in essence pagan, local or national gods, goddesses and heroes. Witchcraft, however, while being a branch of paganism, cannot be merged with Christianity in any way.

WITCHCRAFT

Genuine witchcraft, which is very rare indeed in the twentieth century, is the remnant of a specific Goddess cult that dates back to the dawn of human culture. While it cannot be fused in ritual practice with Christian symbolism, there is no suggestion here that witchcraft is by definition anti-Christian or in any way actively evil. The good or evil of individual practitioners may be open to question, but the pagan cult of the Goddess and her Consort is specifically concerned with the health of the land, animals and humans; it could not, therefore, be based upon a juvenile pseudo-philosophy of antagonism to the powers of Light.

Witchcraft has very specific and narrow limits, and if correctly worked can generate cathartic magical liberation. The true picture of this native cult (in Europe) has been much confused by revival groups; many eccentric or unbalanced people are attracted, and a number of frauds and tricksters make a living from claiming to be witches. So much has been written on the subject that it hardly needs further repetition here, other than to add that western witchcraft has its worldwide parallels, many of which have never been politically vilified and suppressed.

In our context of magical arts, it must be stated that while witchcraft is a true sub-tradition of great antiquity, other magical traditions reach into realms of consciousness and inner worlds not known to witches. Nor is it demanded of any particular cult or tradition that it be all-inclusive or authoritative; certain practices (such as witchcraft) gain tremendous power from their selected limitations. In the advanced magical arts of the present and future, individuals from differing traditions work together without childish conflict; in rituals of this sort early cults such as witchcraft represent aspects of the cultural history of human consciousness, and perform roles that no other type of magician could undertake. If we want our car repaired we do not go to a baker, but a collection of specialisms combine to make both car and bread and deliver food to the hungry.

HERMETICISM

The Hermetic tradition is the intellectual philosophical fusion of the wisdom of ancient cultures[10]. In this sense, it never ceases to grow, for the wisdom of every century is inevitably added to it. There is strong scientific and mathematical emphasis in much Hermetic magic, though this direction was less apparent in early cultures where science and art were not separated. Technical matters relating to magic are learned from Hermetic innerworld contacts; to a limited extent we can say that books on magic, such as this one, are all Hermetic texts. The balancing power to that of Hermes is sometimes said to be Orpheus, the singer who descended into the UnderWorld; and in a magical adept both polarities must be present and ideally equal.

Alchemy and astrology are Hermetic sciences; without Hermetic traditions there would be no modern physics, biology, medicine, science or astronomy. The essential difference between genuine Hermetic tradition and modern occultism is that the invigorating fusion of art-science is giving way to an emasculating fusion of science-psychology.

MODERN OCCULTISM

At its best modern occultism is a development of the Hermetic tradition, though in the broadest sense it includes all magical practices of any sort. Psychology is a type of materialist logical occultism; revealing that which is hidden in the human psyche. Many modern schools of magic have rushed to espouse psychology; this is particularly prevalent in astrology, which has undergone a remarkable revival in this century. There is a constant tendency to take the *magic* out of esoteric practices, justifying them through analogies to science, or through the reductionism of psychology. This approach may be valuable in destroying idle superstition, but genuine magical work always moves inwards; it cannot be rationalised or justified or 'proven' by outwardly directed systems of analysis. Magic is experiential, not intellectual.

Modern occultism is a mixture of nineteenth-century literary occultism with the social psychological sciences; but behind this facade struggling to gain recognition and respectability, there is still magic.

In a later section of this book, the future of magical arts is discussed; in our present context it seems likely that no amount of pseudo-science (para-psychology, telekinesis, telepathy, psychosynthesis) or jargon will obscure true magic. No matter how many new words and money-earning, grant-justifying systems are proliferated, they do little more than re-state qualities and abilities of human consciousness/energy that have always been well-known in magical traditions.

ESOTERIC CHRISTIANITY

Magical ritual has always played an important role in those branches of Christian tradition which were systematically suppressed by the developing political Roman Church, and to a lesser extent by the older orthodox Christian churches in the East. Esoteric Christianity is not really a collection of so-called heresies, but a set of varied practices drawing upon mystical and magical innerworld contacts. If people accept the inner spiritual reality of Christ as the Saviour, but choose to relate to Him through specific forms of ritual or meditation or symbolism, this is esoteric Christianity. It differs from cultism in that it draws upon enduring traditions of mystical or metaphysical symbolism; traditions which may have been suppressed on earth, but still live on in the realms of reality and purified imagination. The best-known example in the west is that of the Grail legends, which fuse pagan Celtic magic with Christian salvation. Other branches of esoteric Christianity also exist; all such branches fuse harmonically with paganism, there is no rejection or conflict, but a universal acknowledgement of mutual understanding.

If we draw a loose correspondence between the Worlds or modes of Being, and the innerworld patterns from Earth to Stars, the various magical traditions fit within specific areas.

ESOTERIC CHRISTIANITY	A UNIVERSAL SAVIOUR:	STELLAR-SOLAR WORLD
HERMETIC OCCULTISM & PAGANISM	KNOWLEDGE OF REALITY IN HUMAN/ TRANSHUMAN TERMS:	SOLAR-LUNAR WORLD
WITCHCRAFT	MAGICAL MOTHERHOOD OF LAND:	LUNAR-EARTH WORLD
UNDERWORLD	DIRECT TRANSFORMA- TION:	EARTH-STELLAR WORLD

It is interesting to note that the UnderWorld Magic and the esoteric Christian intuition merge together within the Earth; a spiritual transformation symbolised by Christ's descent into the lowermost worlds to liberate souls; later propagandised as the 'Harrowing of Hell'.

THE GREAT MOTHER

Understanding, the key word to this chapter, is the property of consciousness which enfolds and enables Wisdom. Traditionally it is symbolised by the Great Mother, she who is at once the vast depths of space and time that enfold and enable the stars, and the Mother of our consciousness and personal understanding. Above the Abyss that separates divine consciousness from human awareness, She is shown as the Third Sphere of the Tree of Life.

The Mother is expressed through all goddess forms; in the higher appearances she is concerned with severity and transformation, while the appearances close to the outer world (Venus and Luna) are concerned with sexual regeneration, both physical and non-physical. The Great Mother is also the Earth Mother, in whom all powers are vested; mystically the Father and Mother are united by the planet and its constant cycle of life.

When a magical Circle is drawn, or a sphere visualised around the magician to contain and refine energies, this is an action of the

Mother. She is the Vessel of all being; in her the energies are shaped to create the Son of Light...the Redeemer symbolised to us as the Sun or Christ. Magical art is a little repetition of this cosmic creation. (0–1) Out of Silence or the Void, the magician emits the first Breath (of the ritual pattern). (1–2) As an act of will (using perhaps a Sword or Rod) the magician draws a circle to represent the field of the universe reflected on earth. (2–3) This action automatically creates a matrix (mother) to receive and restrict the energies that rush forth.

From this stage onwards, the Fourfold pattern (shown in our various diagrams) defines the cycle of energy, and the enlightenment of the magician is due to the presence of the Redeemer or Son of Light, a centrality of consciousness that lives in all Being.

The manifestation of Spheres 4–5, 6, 7–8, 9 and 10 is a process of reflection and progressive expression of energies. By the time they reach 10, the Kingdom, they flow out through the physical body of the magician.

This short summary of the traditional theory of magic should not cause us to follow rigid patterns; spiritual understanding is flexible and infinitely creative, and there are many secret paths to the Mother hidden within the forest of thorns that guards her sanctuary.

9 THE PHILOSOPHY OF COMPASSION

Magical philosophy, or what might be simply called the magical worldview, is holistic. We do not necessarily identify this worldview with the fashionable use of the word holistic currently linked to a number of environmental and health orientated trends; modern restatements or misapplications of the concept of holism are fragmented or even devolved variants of an ancient magical worldview.

In magic, any part contains the essence of any whole in which that part exists; yet the whole is never a mere sum of all the parts. The symbols used in magical rituals are similar to holograms, which are now familiar to almost everyone through laser and photographic developments in art. We could suggest that magical symbols are the holograms of conscious-energy; they mirror a greater entity, truth or image in fragments or viewpoints which nevertheless preserve a specific entire image of the original from which they are apparently separated.

In traditional terminology, the Microcosm reflects the Macrocosm; the consciousness of humankind reflects the consciousness of the Universe.

Many people find their way into magical art through their intuition that the world is not made up of warring disparate entities struggling for the ultimate goal of evolution and survival of the fittest. Through the experiences gained in magical arts we can begin to perceive the holisms, the holograms which reveal a remarkable interconnection between life and consciousness, energy and matter[11].

When the student moves beyond the superficial areas in which the popular absurdities of 'black magic' and 'the occult' may be found festering, he or she soon discovers that powerful magic is based upon very firm ethical foundations. Due to the holistic nature of the world and worlds, we cannot commit evil through magic without damaging ourselves; while it is possible to hide from the awareness of such damage through egotistical delusion, it is not possible to avoid it. Conversely, magical ritual based upon compassion flows forth to benefit many, potentially the whole world; this includes the magician.

This realisation is paradoxical, and many initiates struggle with it for years before growing beyond the paradox; you may not work a ritual based upon compassion which has an ultimate end of self-benefit. You only fool yourself if you try work of this sort. Yet if you work a ritual successfully based upon compassion, you assuredly benefit from it.

There is a well-established subtle science in the direction of consciousness through meditation and ritual. It appears clearly stated in the edited fragments of the New Testament found in the orthodox Bibles, and in greater detail in the prolific but confusing texts of Hermetic magical or metaphysical traditions. This science is less well preserved in the genuine remnants of paganism (not including modern revival paganism which comes from a variety of literary sources) but appears in great depth and detail in medieval texts connected to Merlin, Arthur and the Quest for the Grail.

Once a realisation has been made that the individual is part of the world, no false isolation or separation may be maintained without serious inner damage, or even physical illness. The modern epidemic of stress-related diseases is merely a variant proof of this basic magical law. Such realisation is the catalyst for a most difficult phase for the initiate or student; the superficial habits and requirements of personality constantly feud with the inner direction of the spiritual awareness. No book, group, therapy, or teacher can give any help whatsoever with this conflict; it has to be experienced fully and finally grown out of, passed beyond. The traditional corrective for such problems is meditation and magical ritual based upon compassion. The ultimate aim of spiritual growth is the transformation of conflict and suffering through all worlds; not soothing or mere alleviation, but transformation.

Advanced magical programmes include patterns stretching over long time periods; these may be as short as one lifetime, or of thousands of years' duration. If anyone doubts that such patterns can endure, let them consider the two thousand years of political Christianity and its complex programmes of mass conditioning resulting today in materialism, capitalism, atheism. Once the spirit had been deliberately withheld, and the sexual polarity wilfully perverted, the political religion could only lead in devolutionary directions, destroying itself en route.

. Magical work brings us into contact with a number of other enduring programmes, both pagan and Christian, only a step away from the chaos of the outer world. Such programmes or patterns are aspects of the philosophy and practice of holism within the imagination of orders or groups of entities. Not only is the material world a holistic entity, but the immaterial, imaginative inner worlds all have harmonic cycles of inter-relationship. Such cycles were often symbolised in musical analogies by the Hermetic scientists, alchemists and metaphysicians.

Compassion is not just a matter of sympathy, empathy or even of selfless spiritual love. Sympathy hardly comes into magic at all, especially in the form of sentiment. Sympathy in magic, in the sense of an emotional sentimental bond may cause enormous problems of over-personalising the magical aim; similar to the much discussed psychic phenomena of transference. Spiritual love is a different power altogether, and must not be confused with personal love or sentiment. Mystics and magicians have constantly stated that spiritual love is a terrifying power, burning with an intensity that most of us may not bear without difficulty or even damage. Such power is far removed indeed from the weak notions of unity and intellectual sympathy found in popular 'spiritual' movements.

Compassion is an energy of consciousness that is relatively safe in magic; it is beyond personal emotion or mere sentiment, superior to sympathy; but it also mediates and filters the intensity of the primal fire of Love-as-a-Power. The polarised relationship between compassion or mercy, and severity or justice, is crucial in ritual magic; this relationship is displayed upon the Tree of Life, and beginners think that the two polarities are opposites. Both, in fact, derive from a higher spiritual power of unity; both fuse together to make Harmony or Beauty, the central solar sphere; both are aspects of spiritual love.

In personal terms we might see such energies as positive (compassion) and negative (severity) but this is a very limited viewpoint indeed. Spiritual compassion is of an order of awareness that very few humans achieve; it transcends personality, family, or race; and may seem very severe indeed to those who are unable to understand it. In sexual terms, the polarities are found as male and female, but sexuality in magical art is not limited to mere physical gender, and is seldom defined by mere sensuality.

In the classical Mysteries, the greatest god of all was sometimes said to be Eros, the power of love. This suggests that the interplay between polarities (sexes) runs through all creation, from stars to stones. The flow of these sexual energies in the human and natural world is discussed in later chapters.

How, it may be asked, is the concept and power of compassion enacted in magical ritual and work? The most commonplace formulae are those in which rituals are conducted in the name of a higher power or spiritual being. In orthodox rituals in religion, these beings are God, Christ, Buddha, Allah, Brahma and so on through the world pantheon of names and aspects of ultimate Being. In magic these same figures are often named, but with the added development of finely-tuned specific images. This is equivalent to the professional musician using a hand-made instrument rather than turning on a record player, or the surgeon employing a scalpel rather than dishing out tranquillisers. All such expressions partake of the same essences (music in the first and therapy in the second analogy) yet they are very different indeed in operation and effect, regardless of the ultimate connection between them. It is such refinement that is found in magical art; this quality and practice sets it apart from general worship, even from generalised meditation or spiritual exercises, even though both play a major part in ritual and magical training.

Compassion is placed high upon the Tree of Life (Figure 3); it is a universal power, not a mere concept. It flows towards humans from the higher worlds of conscious-energy, yet we are able to partake of it due to our 'holographic' nature. If the magician or group cannot arouse sufficient degree of this power alone, we act in the name of a higher divinity or God or Goddess-form. Ultimately magic is performed in the name of Divine love, the power of Being that lies at the root of the Universe. Yet to state this aloud initially is to return to the vague realm of generalised spiritual sentiment, or at best to the umbrella of a world religion. Magic gives actual experience of the powers of consciousness and energy, so the training and vocabulary must be very specific indeed. Generalisations weaken magic, even though this creates an apparent paradox when we know that magic is founded upon general unity or holism.

ROLE-REVERSAL IN MAGIC

Magical work is based entirely upon polarity; it is enabled by an all-encompassing permeating energy that polarises through sets of qualities or paths; these paths are manifest to our consciousness as interactions between relatively defined extremes or powers, such as the Elements, or the Spheres upon the Tree of Life.

The power of compassion is one of the classic examples of role-reversal in magic, for once the magical worldview has been generated many of the stereotypes which are hung upon gender come radically adrift. While the customary stereotypes of love and compassion are often female, and the stereotypes of severity male, in the inner workings of magical power these roles are reversed. The innerworld images of compassion are masculine or outgoing and positive, while the images of severity are feminine or ingoing and negative.

The lack of a feminine element in western religion (which is historically a middle-eastern religion imposed upon native western consciousness by force of arms) makes this matter very confusing for the student. Practical experience is usually the best way to come to grips with the matter of role-reversal in magic.

Here is where the Tree of Life, in its gradually changing westernised format, is most valuable, particularly for the student who is not familiar with polarity and role-reversal through native western myth and legend. The Tree is made up of Triads: Male/Female/Neutral. Every time a power is encountered upon a new dimension or plane, it may change sexual imagery; which really means that it changes polarity.

The would-be magician must always be aware that such changes are inevitable, not only in images encountered within the tuned imagination, but within himself or herself. The true nature of the human being is androgynous, a central entity with perfectly-balanced powers cycling harmoniously; the Triads of the Tree of Life show three levels of this balance:

1) Being, Wisdom, Understanding.
2) Beauty, Severity, Mercy.
3) Foundation, Victory, Honour (or Glory).

These are respectively:

1) A universal triad of all encompassing awareness.
2) A transcendent triad of power.
3) A living triad of generative, emotional and mental energies.

The initiations and transformations found in magical tradition aim to establish an understanding relationship with triadic patterns, and to shape the individual energies accordingly.

Compassion is the highest level of consciousness before the

universal Abyss; it is the most potent power that may be filtered through to the human state in the outer world; its operation cuts across all other cycles and powers, if we are once able to achieve the polar state required for its effective transmission into the outer realms.

10 DISCIPLINE

One of the most unacceptable propositions regarding magic, to both the would-be magician and the sceptic, is that the art demands very rigorous and specific disciplines. Discipline in general is an unavoidable requirement in magic, combining the skills of art, craft and science, projecting attention into new areas of perception and operation. Both the popular picture of magic being easy, a picture enhanced by the rash of trivial jovial lightweight books that claim to teach the subject, and the fictional concept of magic harnessing unhallowed powers to cheat a way through life, are untrue.

There is no power without restriction; no control of power without a controlling matrix; in magic the matrix is not merely a construct or pattern developed in training, it is our entire entity... ourselves. In early stages of training we perceive constructs and symbols as if they are exterior, while in later stages we know them to be inner realities; but the aim of magical art is to fuse the inner and outer perceptions into a whole rhythmic reality, of which the body and psyche are inseparable elements regardless of our wordplay used to describe them.

It has often been said that the required list of disciplines for the magician reads like an idealised definition of a superman or woman; we may never fully achieve such ends, and if we do so they are transformed and have no trace of their original temporal value; but we may always work towards them. The list includes: patience; perseverance; compassion; self-control; discipline in all aspects of the inner and outer life and habits; cleanliness (absolutely essential for magical work); physical fitness; effort at study and expansion of knowledge. All of these are the supporting cast for the main disciplines of concentration, meditation, visualisation and ritual pattern making.

83

INITIATION AND DISCIPLINE

The much-discussed and little-understood subject of 'initiation' is built almost entirely around the cumulative effect of discipline and its binding and releasing of energies within the individual. Initiation emphatically does not consist of powers mysteriously conferred upon us during vague quasi-religious ceremonies...it cannot work in this manner. Initiation may be described as a matter of very basic physics, or perhaps we could invent a term and say psycho-physics, a lesser harmonic of metaphysics. Magic deals exclusively with knowledge of psycho-physical laws, leading towards spiritual realisation.

The normal flow of our life-energies is wasteful, vague, disorientated, habitual, and devoid of intent. This is true not only of the stereotypical 'average man and woman' but applies also to strong driving personalities, who are enslaved by the habit of achievement and power-seeking, lacking any vision of worlds beyond their self-imposed limits. By restricting our habitual flow and direction of attention and energy (no matter what form or lack of form it takes), and directing the flow into a harmonic matrix of consciousness/energy, which is a magical tradition or coherent set of symbols for inner transformation, we build up pressure. This pressure is not superficial emotional tension, but a rising level of life energy shaped by the matrices of the magical disciplines and symbols; the same energy might normally be directed towards habitual ends or merely be dissipated. In training, the normal energies are redirected; this often gives an illusion of higher levels of energy, but these truly arise in advanced magical work.

During initiation, a door is opened, or a gate created, both within the individual psyche and in imaginal (but not imaginary or false) worlds, through which the pressurised or shaped energies of the initiate are channelled. The essential difference between magic and other schools of inner growth and transformation is the use of worlds and dimensions in which the magician is transformed through a series of encounters; initiation (which merely means *beginning*) is the traditional process by which the individual starts off on his or her inner journey through such worlds. Literary occultism, locked into the male-stereotypical fantasy of 'merit' and 'authority', frequently advises us of grades and levels of initiation (ensuring, of course, that teachers and leaders have *higher grades* than other members of any group). In truth there is only one initiation, and if we were able to relate to it entirely at our first experience all subsequent art of magic would be unnecessary. In practice, however, we unfold and

84

encounter the various harmonics of initiation through what appears to be a series of encounters and inner changes.

Discipline, and the universal power of catalysis or breakdown that underpins human discipline, firstly restricts the personalised energies within a new matrix or magical tradition. The disciplines also enable the initiate to remain true to his or her intention during the moment of initiation. The first perception of the Gate of initiation is gained through dissolution of the habitual conditioned personality; there is no easy way of handling this experience. Popularised systems or schools that claim magical or meditative arts to be 'gentle' are either deliberately misleading, or taught by those who have no experience of the subject within themselves, but merely a literary or social/psychological background. Many so-called experts can exist for years without ever experiencing a true magical initiation; the hallmark of such people is that they live off others, both materially and psychically, reinforcing their patterns through social groups and a parade of gullible students.

But we can balance the grim picture of magical discipline with a certain knowledge; after breakdown, catalysis, comes the balancing power that restructures. The newly liberated energies take on a pattern of simplicity, of health, or of harmony. This type of magical transformation has nothing to do with 'powers' or selfish ends; it gives a new worldview in which properties of consciousness/energy are released to act in their proper modes, rather than be weakened through habitual cycles of limitation. Paradoxically, it is the discipline, the replacing of illusory limitation with a willed set of controls, that brings initiation and subsequent liberation. In legendary terms, this process is symbolised by the quest for the Grail, which is a vessel of perpetual regeneration, guarded by terrors and wonders that can and often do destroy the seeker. But the destruction is that of the false personality; the Grail then regenerates the initiate, brings him or her back from the dead.

Initiates are traditionally known as the living dead, or the twice born, those who have seen the sun at midnight. Such poetical terms describe an actual *event*, a moment of resonance in the lifetime which unfolds as a state of consciousness only after its temporal occurrence. In the classical Mysteries, initiations were carried through by a firm set of disciplines culminating in a ceremony or cycle of ceremonies. The initiation itself arose from the combination of inner and outer disciplines and the ritual pattern which located a Gate or moment of transformation in both space and time. By ritual, we formally define the event of initiation; but the ritual is meaningless nonsense without the disciplines and traditional arts that it focuses.

The same situation is found today; no magical initiation has any value if it is merely a show devoid of background and effort. What actually occurs during such ceremonies is very simple: the experienced members of the group order or Mystery act as mediators between the worlds. The initiate must pass through the Gate alone, but all the necessary conditions, and the vital innerworld contacts are unified by the ritual pattern employed. In other words it is not the ritual that confers initiation, but initiation that generates the ritual.

QUALITIES AND ASPECTS OF DISCIPLINE

At the opening of this chapter, there is a random list of some of the qualities required of the magician; there are others that will be added during our discussion. Before proceeding further, it should be stated that these qualities are not 'virtues'; there is no moral or religious superiority implied. The qualities are *essential basics* and not the signs or benefits of being a wonderful person who lives a meaningful life. Magic continually destroys self-inflation, and there is no implication that the basic qualities are anything more than training and tuning requirements. In orthodox religious systems such qualities are given inherent value as a means of encouraging the faithful to live according to a pattern, or more perniciously to indoctrinate them for the benefit of the religious hierarchy. In magical traditions the initiate is trained to live through a harmonic series of patterns without taking any one as being the ultimate value or reality; truth is found through transformation and regeneration rather than through acquisition of required virtues.

Bearing firmly in mind, therefore, that there is no score of merit in magical development, we can examine some of the qualities and disciplines essential to magical arts.

Patience

Patience is the essential requirement for any science art or skill. We do not expect to play a musical instrument in a day, or invent technologies or artifacts without background, skill, training and study. Patience is more essential in magic than in any other activity, and we do not mean the spurious 'patience' of submission to oppression and abuse from authority. Such abuses of society and individuality may indeed be valuable to the magician to encounter as training material in patience and discipline, but patience has no virtue of its own right, it only has a value in specific contexts. There are, in other words, times when action must balance patience. Each quality or inner discipline has a shadow, a perversion which creeps in either through abuse or through excessive development of one specific attitude without its balancing factors. Patience, humility, acceptance and meekness have been used as cloaks for many centuries to hide direct mental emotional and spiritual abuse of humankind.

Patience must be based upon the premise that an end is anticipated, a goal known to exist; but in the wisdom tradition worldwide it is the process or transformation arising through *seeking* that is of value, and not the goal sought after so patiently. In magical work, patience is linked to an increasing understanding of cycles; flowers cannot be easily forced to grow in winter, which is part of the planetary cycle around the sun, which in turn is part of a stellar cycle or rotation. Patience, discipline and supportive knowledge enable the initiate to become aware of cycles of life; and to wait for events to flower at their proper time. The patience with which we are concerned in magic is not an intellectual or rational formula; it is organically derived from traditions and knowledge of the relationship between inner and outer worlds.

When it becomes a matter of true perception (rather than mere theory) patience is linked to meditation and intuition upon rebirth, upon renewal, and the resonance of patterns through time. Many of the exercises employed in magical training are ultimately designed to give the initiate this overview that brings genuine patience; it can only come from experience of alternative worldviews, even though its seeds may be planted in everyday disciplines and perseverance.

The organic continuity of magic is found in its remarkable endurance through historical time; the members of a genuine magical order know that the work in hand is not a matter of one hour, one year, or even of one lifetime, but that it is part of a cycle that extends for many lifetimes through many cultural phases. The secret of magical patience is found in not being distracted by the superficial aspects of any one magical ritual or project; there is always a central heart to any magical pattern, a heart from which any number of resonant events may derive. Once this understanding is achieved, the lesser details fall into place. As our life in its entirety is a magical ritual, the value of patience is inestimable.

There are two ways of considering the organic continuity of magic; the first is that magical traditions and related behaviour regenerate due to the inherent nature of the psyche. The second is that such patterns are maintained through the relationships between beings in other worlds or dimensions, and human beings in the outer world. Modern magical arts fuse both viewpoints together, and rely strongly on practical experience rather than continued discussion of theory. If we patiently apply the key symbols of magical tradition, we find that many fresh aspects regenerate within group and individual awareness; we also find that we make innerworld contact with beings who uphold the magical traditions, and who act as guardians for programmes or patterns that endure for very long periods of time. It is at this stage that the magician becomes involved not only with his or her own inner transformation, but with transformative effects upon the human consciousness and the planet in general.

Perseverance

Perseverance is closely linked to Patience, but implies action. It can be a valuable balance for the perverted form of Patience, which is a type of 'spiritualised' vapidness and timelessness, leading ultimately to a very negative state of low energy posing as spirituality and mystical acceptance.

Any craftsman will confirm that there is a living skill that grows only through persevering in the craft; the hands learn to unfold that which the mind alone cannot force through with rational thought. In this sense magic is very close to woodcarving or sculpture; with regular discipline and perseverance we acquire a style and grace in even the simplest inflexion of the work in hand. The raw material, of course, is our living entity, and this type of work is very far removed indeed from the demonic concept of the 'self-made man' or 'improving one's self'.

Many modern people play around with magic at some time in their lives; but because they do not persevere they feel that they have been cheated. It would be no exaggeration to suggest that there are only two major requirements for a magician: patience and perseverance. The rest, which is immeasurable, comes naturally from within our consciousness, providing we undergo the necessary disciplines for redirection of our life energies.

Compassion

Compassion has been dealt with in some detail in our earlier chapters, as it is the central ethic and polarising power of magical work. We may briefly say in the present context that Compassion is the polar balance and partner to Severity, as shown upon the Tree of Life. Human beings require a transpersonal aim to catalyse freedom from the tyranny of the false personality; discipline will carry us far indeed, but one step beyond discipline is compassion. Where would-be magicians make repeated mistakes is in seeking the power of Compassion or giving before undergoing the purification of discipline or Taking.

Self-Discipline

This may range from the absurdities of the fakir to the daily qualities of restraint and maturity required for sharing life with other people, no matter how insanely dangerous or pettily selfish they may seem to be. In magic the disciplines are means towards an end, and not ends in themselves. The most important tools for the developing magician are not, paradoxically, meditation or visualisation, for these powers will blossom from their true roots quite spontaneously if we give them the opportunity. What is required is discipline in apparently small or even trivial matters; matters which directly affect the imagination, the psycho-physical energies, and the sensitivity to the holisms that are at work in magical ritual.

In the modern context these disciplines include many restrictions which run contrary to the mainstream of psychic flow; less or no television, no video games or computer toys, no loud electronic music or flashing lights. None of this implies a rejection of modern culture, but suggests controlled involvement through awareness of areas that distract, confuse, trivialise or even damage the inner faculties. Disciplines in matters of sensuality or sexuality have always been known to be crucial for inner growth, and are dealt with in our later chapters.

Cleanliness

This is obviously a self-discipline, but merits a short section in its own right, as it is a very magical subject indeed. In magical analysis, as opposed to modern psycho-analysis, dirt is an outer manifestation of an inner imbalance. Unfortunately the corollary does not hold true; outer cleanliness is not necessarily a sign of inner balance, it can easily be a posture or merely a conditioned habit.

Magic works by analogy; the disciplines of clean body and clean house contribute towards inner health, particularly when the individual is involved in magical work. If the boundaries between inner and outer worlds are firmly shut, clean habits will not go far towards inner purification, but once we start upon the path of magical transformation, outer conditions become paradoxically important.

On a less superficial level than that of personality analysis, we should always be aware that the initiatory powers of consciousness/energy are intimately connected to concepts of purification, transformation, and rebalance. Many self-acclaimed magicians go through periods in which they strongly resist and fight against the very changes that magic causes; this willed inner sloth manifests as chaos in the personal living habits, and indulgence in unnecessary relationships and situations with a superficially 'magical' ambience. Magic, more than any other self-acclaimed inner discipline, seeks to bring clarity and simplicity into the world; replacing chaos with balance, bringing confused awareness through into increased perception.

As magic works by analogy, the magical practitioner who revels in dirt is actually strengthening his or her inner pollution by a surrounding set of circumstances that mirror and amplify inner weakness.

Physical Health

The requirement of physical fitness is central to magical work, particularly in the delicate matter of keeping the blood free of toxins. In advanced magical arts, the bloodstream is transformed in very subtle ways, with biochemical changes arising through the intimate link between our imagination, our life energies, and our overall physical entity[12]. Modern people are familiar with such concepts from orthodox chemical and medical research, in which chemotherapy is applied to alter consciousness, usually in the emotional realm or mode. A magical and mystical tradition regarding blood chemistry has been known for many centuries, couched in poetic and religious terminology or the symbolic language of the Mysteries; such knowledge is by no means a modern discovery. Many of the dietary requirements of inner traditions are not merely matters of health or compassion, but of subtle changes in the bloodstream which are augmented by meditative and ritual practices.

IMBALANCE, DISORIENTATION AND DRUGS

During the nineteenth century, in the great upsurge of so-called spiritualism and intellectual Theosophy, there was a widespread notion (often found in modern publications today) that a 'spiritual' person was physically inept, sick or even disabled. This is simply untrue; people of all ranges of ability or disability may enter into magical or inner work and discipline; a physical imbalance emphatically does not act as a directive for energies towards inner realms. Such doctrines are merely an ignorant perversion of the laws of polarity and energy-exchange employed in the enduring wisdom traditions. Such teachings were combined with the woeful corruption of Christian orthodoxy, in which the body was taught to be a source of sin and evil; if the body was mortified then the spirit was free! In magical art this has never been taught or practised in the west, and students with reasonably healthy bodies should not pursue paths of imbalance or disorientation in order to work magic. There are traditions that employ such means, but the price is very high to pay.

The ultimate price of such short-cut methods is an inner decay or imbalance that may be carried over from one lifetime to another, extending beyond the obvious abuse of the physical body. A typical modern example would be the use of LSD for alteration of awareness, or the cocaine and heroin usage that destroyed notorious adepts such as Aliester Crowley.

Health in magic is about simple cleanliness of body, psyche and living environment, and not a matter of forced exercises or restrictions or regimens that claim to have miraculous or paranormal effect. We should add briefly that hypnosis, regressive techniques, and similar methods in which the psyche is placed under willed disorientation through the suggestive power of another person are strictly banned in genuine magical traditions.

No member of the western Mysteries will ever offer to regress or hypnotise a student, nor should any student accept such exercises, as their polluting effect takes a long period of time and effort to rebalance. Although such techniques are extremely popular today, even fashionable as a type of sensual experience superficially free of side-effects and ostensibly therapeutic, they are the ragbag of an ancient debased magical system. Magic of this sort, closely linked to phantom allies (spiritualism) and trance mediumship, derives from traditions which are no longer valid or healthy for modern people; in this sense the opposition of the orthodox religions to such activities is fully justified. No matter what system was employed in the distant past that involved regressive hypnotic or somnambulistic techniques, it is long since corrupted and fragmented. Setting all such considerations aside, common sense advises us that such techniques are energy-consuming and degrading to the individual spirit. All of the benefits claimed by occult hypnotic or regressive techniques may be found in full awareness through healthy meditation, without ever placing one's soul under the temporary control of another person's will, or allowing any form of block or conditioning to be imposed upon the habitual consciousness through hypnotic means.

THE AIMS OF MAGICAL DISCIPLINES

What are the aims of magical disciplines? They are, in short, designed to project us into other worlds. This statement should not be taken metaphorically; it is literally a matter of being projected, often with considerable energy, into other worlds. Initially magic alters the focus or area of attention, drawing the vital energies together within the discipline of a tradition and its restricting vessel or matrix. In a second stage, the energies are redirected and gradually amplified through attuning to greater holisms or patterns; this type of magical work is best represented by the Wheel of Life and Change, or the Magical Circle. Thirdly, the awareness, having been attuned to various patterns normally inaccessible to everyday consciousness, begins to operate in other worlds or dimensions through the effect of the magical patterns and key symbols. Finally, the magician is projected into the alternative worlds, not merely in the imagination, but through every aspect of his or her entity. The ultimate transformation of this type is found in magical traditions worldwide, in which certain individuals have physically disappeared into other worlds[13].

What, we may ask, is the point of this type of transition? Curiously the magical traditions do not value the transition from world to world as a mere alternative to consensual experience in the regular world; it is not merely another pleasure trip. The value of the transition is that every time we make such a change of world-reality, we contribute to the overall liberation from illusion or a rigid coagulated worldview. In traditions or orders particularly concerned with education, there is the further benefit that knowledge may be exchanged from world to world; this concept is upheld repeatedly in myth and legend.

Such dynamic transitions cannot be made idly; the training and discipline act to free us from habit and weaknesses in our energy patterns. Only when we have been transformed by the experience of initiation supported by discipline can we begin the more potent level of energetic pattern-making that projects us into other worlds. The worlds are first encountered through the imagination, but ultimately through the agency of the physical body. The classic examples in

British tradition are those people who disappear into Faeryland; the seer and magician Thomas Rhymer and the priest Robert Kirk (both historical persons) are known to have spent timeless time in the Otherworld. Robert Kirk is still said, in his native region of Scotland, to be in Faeryland to this day. The most potent example of this type of transition is found in the figure of Merlin, the fountainhead of British magical traditions.

In a general sense, faith and spiritual intuition can strengthen us for these magical experiences, but only discipline and redirection of our attention and energies can actually enable us to undertake such radical transitions from world to world. The education for such changes comes from tradition; where outer tradition and individual tuition ends or fails, the communication of innerworld teachers becomes essential to the practice of western magic.

MARS AND MINERVA

The Fifth Sphere (Severity) upon the Tree of Life is said to be that in which initiates become major adepts. The entire matter of 'grades' seems rather absurd today, but it contains the kernel of a significant insight into inner growth.

Through the power of Severity all excess baggage is destroyed, and most of this encumbrance is the mask or personality. Regrettably the Fifth Sphere is associated in occult literature with Mars, a militaristic male-dominant image prone to fits of jealous rage and sexual over-possessiveness. Originally this sphere was, and still is, feminine. The ancient goddesses of war and taking, such as the primal 'Minerva' or the Celtic Morrigan, reveal truths far deeper than mere conquest. They destroy to recreate, they break down to heal. The growth of adept abilities is made through the destruction of trivial or imbalanced conditions of inner attention.

This cosmic destroying force, seen as winter on the land or as the life-decay of stars in space, is also the realm or mode of retribution. While Mars represents vengeance or rage, Minerva or Athena represent justice and discipline. The effect of feminine images of discipline is very different from those of male stereotypes; this is proven by meditation and ritual work with such images.

11 HARMONY AND SPIRITUAL ENLIGHTENMENT

There are two major aims of magical ritual and magical inner transformation: the first is to balance and harmonise the holisms or worlds including but transcending the human world; the second is to energise such holisms increasing their rate or level of consciousness in order to transmute utterly into new dimensions. This twofold aim is normally termed the process of spiritual enlightenment, drawing its symbolism from the sun, our star at the centre of the solar world system. In magical terms, the solar system is a world, composed of not only a star and attendant planetary and other bodies, but a series of dimensions and beings that are metaphysical.

During magical development, the two aims within the student are at first divided, operating as separate types of activity. The first, balancing the worlds within individual consciousness, manifests as ritual and planned activity, by which life becomes attuned and rhythmic rather than random and chaotic. The order sought, it must be stressed, is not rigid or static, but one in which all energies are united towards selected ends; primarily towards the transformation of the individual, beginning with the demonic personality and reaching towards the spiritual transcendent awareness that lives within each of us. Through ritual work, the initiate comes into contact with natural life, rebalancing his or herself and establishing relationships with other life forms to create a holistic interaction . . . a better world.

The second aim, energising the constructs established and the contacts provided, consists primarily of transformative rituals and powerful mediation; by such means the spiritual power inherent within us is directed outwards towards material ends; before this can occur it has to flow through the psychic-body complex, transforming the matter and awareness of the magician before it reaches any other defined goal.

These initial two aims soon merge into one harmonious living pattern, a magical life of enlightenment. Here is where magic differs radically from prayer or meditation, for it seeks a continual interaction between the individual and the world or worlds occupied by that individual right through to the physical manifestations. To change the world by magic is to change yourself; your body is literally the world.

THE FOUR WORLDS

The energy employed is that same primal creative/destructive energy breathed forth by the spirit of origination, Being out of Non-Being. This process of differentiation or reflection is traditionally illustrated in four stages, often called four worlds or dimensions of devolution. These stages, shown in our Figure 5, are ORIGINATION: CREATION: FORMATION: EXPRESSION. They are archetypical modes devolving in a series or spiral towards material coagulation.

Each level is increasingly crystallised or concrete as it reflects outwards or downwards form the preceding level. Obviously this fourfold pattern is a conceptual aid, and not necessarily a definitive statement on the nature of Being manifesting out of Non-Being. There are many exceptions to the pattern, not the least of which is a specific path central to western esoteric traditions, in which a being may cut across all and any barriers between the worlds instantaneously.

In general magical work, the series of devolution is seldom strictly adhered to, least of all regarded as dogma. In practice the worlds often fuse together harmonically of their own accord, but the fourfold devolution is a useful teaching aid, giving the consciousness a model to hold in the event of casting adrift upon the sea of Being. There are a number of other models, and most models fuse together to form the ubiquitous Tree of Life.

The fourfold expression corresponds poetically to the magical system found in western culture in several important ways which are worth analysing briefly. One of the best texts for this system is the twelfth-century *Vita Merlini*, as its cosmology is identical to that still taught in magical education today. Although we do not present it as 'proof' of anything at all, the *Vita* makes a historical anchoring point which states that such systems were still active in the medieval period; it is interesting to note that very few modern occultists of the nineteeth and twentieth centuries were aware of this text which was not available in any type of translation until fairly late, and not in

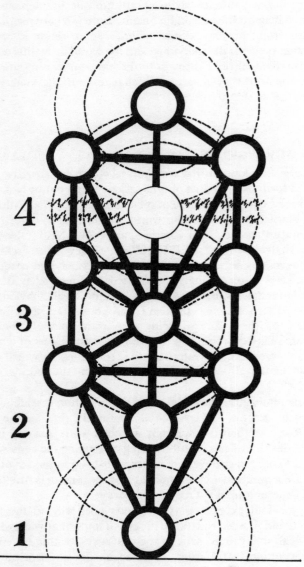

Figure 5. *The Four Worlds upon the Tree of Life.*
4) ORIGINATIVE WORLD: Star World.
3) CREATIVE WORLD: Solar World.
2) FORMATIVE WORLD: Lunar World.
1) EXPRESSIVE WORLD: Earth World.
The Worlds merge harmonically and do not have hard boundaries. Phases described as stellar, solar, lunar and earth act as conceptual models for the energies of Being and should not be taken to mean merely the physical stars through to planet Earth.

complete systematic translation until the twentieth century. It predates the appearance of what is quite wrongly termed 'standard' magical symbolism which is derived from very free interpretations of Hebrew mysticism intermingled with many other sources.

The patterns found in the *Vita* are exactly those of magical art as taught in western inner and esoteric schools, and as handed down through magical orders intermingled with later literary accumulation. The source-system is the oral wisdom tradition of the west, nothing more nor less.

In the Creation sequence taught by the bard Taliesin to the prophet Merlin, the order of manifestation is: STARS, SUN, MOON, EARTH. This would correspond to the idealised modes of devolution mentioned above. It also harmonises with the classical/medieval system of the Four Elements: AIR, FIRE, WATER, EARTH. These elements are higher octaves than physical matter, yet permeate all matter and all non-material worlds, right through to originative levels, by which stage they are the Four Aspects of Being or the cycle of divine consciousness.

The Fourfold Pattern is shown in Figure 6, and is the major symbol used in ritual magic worldwide. The correspondences are as follows:

ORIGINATION	AIR	STARS	(Being is Breathed forth from Unbeing)
CREATION	FIRE	SUN	(Specific stars create worlds)
FORMATION	WATER	MOON	(Life forms are manifested in worlds)
EXPRESSION	EARTH	EARTH	(As specific group-world, and as matter)

These Four stages link to the Four Seasons and the Wheel of Life, shown in Figure 1. The correspondences are:

SPRING	AIR	BIRTH	EAST
SUMMER	FIRE	ADULTHOOD	SOUTH
AUTUMN	WATER	MATURITY	WEST
WINTER	EARTH	AGE	NORTH

The divisions are not rigid but fluid, and capable of an infinite number of combinations. To train the will and imagination of the magician, the inherent abilities of the psyche and the inherent qualities of defined energy in the universe are further symbolised by

Figure 6. *Wheel of Life (II) and Signs of the Zodiac.*
Air: Implement of Sword or Arrow.
Fire: Implement of Rod, Spear or Staff.
Water: Implement of Cup or Cauldron.
Earth: Implement of Shield or Mirror.
Centre: Implement of Lamp or Crystal.

Four Implements; and the divine consciousness by Four Powers or aspects of the cycle of Being;

AIR	SWORD	LIFE
FIRE	ROD	LIGHT
WATER	CUP	LOVE
EARTH	SHIELD	LAW

To each Implement a spiritual power or transcendent quality is attuned, not only through ritual but through the universal pattern that ritual seeks to emulate, the cycle of Life, Light, Love and Law.

We could take the list further and define symbols such as the Tarot Trumps which are used in traditional magical techniques, not for idle 'fortune-telling', but as pictoral symbols for meditation and visualisation. The cards which apply are STAR, SUN, MOON, and the Four Aces. Ultimately the entire pack is manifested out of these primary relationships.

The basics of magic are, therefore, relatively simple and few. This theme of complexity out of simplicity holds good in every field of our comprehension, from mathematics to biology.

The advantage of primal symbolism is that, if we are able to attune the system correctly, the more complex aspects automatically or harmonically appear. Magic works from the inside outwards, right through to physical manifestation.

Science, on the other hand, works from outside inwards, gaining remarkable results by only reaching as far as the reasoning faculties with occasional flashes of intuition. The intellectual sphere is relatively close to the material world, and most of us are locked into repeated channels or paths between intellect, emotion and physical sexuality, the three lowermost spheres of energy upon the Tree of Life (see Figure 7). These spheres merge into the outer world or tenth sphere, which is both the planet and the body of humankind, and has a cosmic level as all manifested matter.

We seldom take that small but important step that carries us one world further, into the realm of spiritual enlightenment, harmony and balance, which immediately transcends the other four. This area of consciousness is symbolised by the Sun, or the solar system in magical tradition. In modern psychology it sometimes is admitted as a transpersonal aspect of the psyche, while in physics it is the source of the energy released by nuclear (stellar) reactions. Our society draws upon the physical release of such energies without the corresponding spiritual consciousness; it is a type of theft for which we are already paying an incalculable price.

The solar or balanced creative/destructive consciousness is one of the main achievements sought by the magician.

RELIGIOUS AND MYSTICAL IMAGES OF HARMONY

In world religions the realm of harmony, the solar world, is the dimension of the great Saviours, the enlightened ones, the saints, or the solar heroes. They form bridges between the stellar consciousness of the sun and its worlds and inhabitants; they also commune with the consciousness of other stars and worlds. The relevant reality of such figures is discussed in our chapter on innerworld contacts, but we may recognise that regardless of their actual nature such

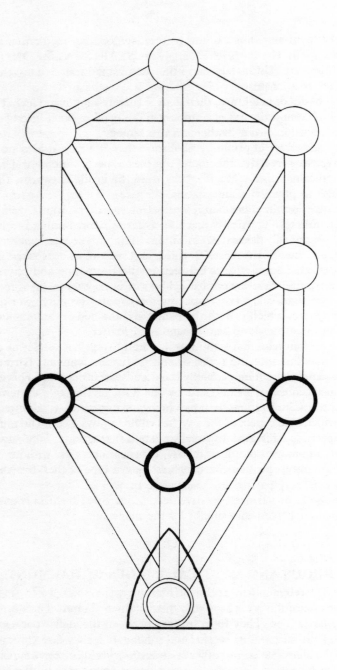

Figure 7. Polarity of Lower Spheres.

divinities or transhuman beings resonate within the human consciousness if allowed to come into contact.

Christ, Buddha, and the pagan sun-kings and heroes merge together in this world of consciousness; yet the first two Saviours also transcend it and bridge through to the stellar universe, while the sun-kings and heroes are pertinent to the solar and sub-solar world of humans. This centrality, power in poise, is also attainable as a psychic quality, a state reflecting and partaking of the solar world, reached by meditation and ritual. The key word is *balance,* and the awareness that balances perfectly is filled with light.

Just as the physical solar system has its sun/star at the heart of its entity or world, so does each human being have a reflection of this centre within. Technically there are two manifestations of centrality; one is a purely spiritual reality within us all, while the other is an energetic network of power centres equated with stars, sun and moon in traditional magic, but existing within the human entity and corresponding to energies defined by the four worlds. The harmonious fusion of the power centres or assemblies of energy with the spiritual seed or centrality is the ultimate aim of one major magical initiation; it is also the aim of religious and mystical translation from a merely human condition to union with divinity.

To put this more simply, just as the Sun has a spiritual Being or metaphysical sun that it reflects, so do we have a solar centre within our consciousness/energy field, which reflects that same spiritual being according to our limited capacity to relate to such a Being. The Saviour figures, found in this Sixth Sphere of the Tree of Life, or solar world, or realm of Harmony, are a human interface between outer humanity and inner Being. They partake of both humanity and divinity, hence their role as Saviours, Bridge-keepers or Redeemers.

MAGICAL RITUAL AND HARMONY

In ceremony, physical ritual, patterns are drawn. These patterns help to direct our consciousness/energy towards holisms or units of integrated energy which have the power of transformation. One of the most important of such holisms is the Sphere of Harmony or Beauty, and its associated Saviours and sacred kings.

Magicians may use the pattern-making or ritual and its power to build bridges through to holisms or unified worlds of consciousness; they use it primarily to retune themselves, sometimes in surprising and dynamic ways. Eventually the concept of retuning and harmonising one's self merges with a series of innerworld programmes or projects. These long-term programmes are generated by higher forms of consciousness and relate to the environment, and to further union between the inner and outer worlds.

Paradoxically, although magical arts acknowledge the power of the Saviour, they do not assume that the world is saved merely by believing. Belief is the first stage of a long process which develops into true spiritual mediation of the redeeming energies of the Saviour; this is the meaning of the ancient tradition of the kingly order of Melchizadek found in the Old Testament, but also found culturally worldwide wherever souls develop a harmonious spiritual tradition of transformation and redemption.

Under certain initiatory circumstances, the magician moves beyond the Sphere of Harmony; there are five further spheres upon the Tree of Life, and the entire universe of stellar worlds. But for most of us the achievement of genuine physical, psychic and spiritual harmony is a goal that may take not one but many lifetimes.

This achievement may be glimpsed, however, or even attained, within an instant; such instants are one of the major aims of magical initiation. Magic can create a through-line, a flow, in which all energies are suddenly harmonised from stellar to solar to lunar and planetary consciousness, both within and without the human entity. Astrology originated with this type of magical work, and was never really concerned with trivial prediction or even psychic mapping such as it undertakes today. In early magical art, astrological patterns were defined and used to synchronise inner and outer events linked harmonically through the various worlds. We find a vague remnant of this tradition in the appearance of the Star of Bethlehem and the three astrologers (also kings) who sought the divine child among the Elemental creatures in the stable.

To conclude our short section upon Harmony we must always remember that the central images, the Saviour or sacred kings, may be either merciful or severe. There is very dangerous tendency to assume that such beings are sweetness as well as light; the cosy glow of pseudo-religious vapid spirituality plays no part in the true realisation of the Son of Light.

12 EMOTIONS AND IMAGINATION

Magic is difficult to prove in materialist terms, despite the fact that branches of magical art, especially the Hermetic and alchemical and cosmological traditions, created modern science; their profound effects may still be traced in materialist conceptual models that are superficially removed from a magical worldview.

As we have repeatedly affirmed, magic is concerned with the forces of the imagination. There is no single definition of magic, but throughout this book various inter-related definitions are offered; the true value of each changes with inner transformation of the magician. In our context of the imagination we could say that magic is an artistic science designed to energise the imagination. It does so to such an extent that it transforms the relationship between consciousness and material expression. In simpler words, magic changes things inwardly and outwardly.

The imagination, the faculty of consciousness which produces images, runs through all Four Worlds, Four Elements, Ten Spheres. It is not limited to fanciful entertainment, but ultimately the human imagination is a fragment of that vast imagination which enfolds the universe; the universe which we perceive and tally is an image of a reality that we cannot fully comprehend. This last definition might not be too unacceptable to a modern physicist.

In magical training work, which persists from student to most advanced levels, both the imagination and the emotions are employed to generate changes of consciousness, physical and biological reactions, and in the breakdown of coagulated encrusted layers of habit, delusion and indifference. It is this practical use of imagination linked to emotional reaction that is the theme of our chapter; other uses of imagination are dealt with elsewhere.

Most of us are familiar either consciously or unconsciously with wilful abuse of imagination and emotion; such abuse is found at political rallies, revivalist or enthusiastic religious meetings, commercial pseudo-eastern cults for the gullible western consumer, football matches, rock concerts, even the fetishistic materialist wedding ceremony (once connected to the Christian religion); all generate unnatural emotion or misdirect natural valuable emotions for spurious, corrupt or even dangerous ends. In magical art an overview of emotional conditioning and control is attained through meditation upon the true qualities of the images employed in such abuses, but the magician seeks to turn the power inwards towards spiritual reality and truth rather than outwards towards illusion and confusion.

The techniques of magic, however, are basically the same techniques as are applied crudely by popular manipulators of emotion. But in magical art the techniques are refined and harmonised for very selective ends; to transform the consciousness and liberate it from the abuse and degradation of emotional slavery. Such abuse includes many forms more subtle than those crude and obvious examples listed above.

Enduring traditions of magical psychology, which long pre-date materialist studies of the psyche, have always employed sets of images to generate emotion. Magic also generates other energies, which are discussed in our other chapters. Magical images employed in emotional context are similar to the so-called archetypes of modern psychology, but the term archetype is applied in a very specific manner in magic and metaphysics, while generalised modern usage is misappropriated from its true source. An archetype is, and has always been, a universal matrix for a wide spectrum of energies of which consciousness in the human psyche is merely one reflection; an archetype is not, and never has been, merely a coherent or enduring image found within the psyche.

The images used in magic are basically derived from those shared by the collective imagination; they are found in myth, legend, folklore, the primal relationships of humanity to the land and to other entities, and eventually lead to reflection upon the mysteries of existence in all worlds. It is only on this last level that the images may be truly identified with archetypes, by which stage many of the preceding forms have disappeared or become redundant.

When such images are refined and specifically attuned to selected forces or energies, they become *magical* images. A magical image is a finely-made tool for consciousness, yet it has a life and energy uniquely its own, and may even encapsulate independent consciousness in its own right. Such a definition would have been less acceptable twenty or thirty years ago than it is today; the use of computer technology has demonstrated on a mass popular level that there are clear analogies between consciousness and artificial structures that perform functions originally limited to the human mind. Magical images are emphatically not computers, they do not work in the same manner as computers, nevertheless they are models of functional design that interact with human awareness to obtain pre-defined results. Push the correct buttons and a known reaction occurs, though its final expression will often contain surprises.

Such images are used in magic to stimulate and alter the emotions. There is a bizarre tendency in esoteric work to decry emotion, as if it is a weakness. Some of this imbalanced attitude is the product of the male-stereotype in political mono-sexual religion; it has been compounded by the influence of old-fashioned literary occultism deriving from gross misunderstanding of Buddhism and other eastern practices in which the emotions are brought under conscious control in the early training stages. Emotion plays a major role in magic, as it does in mystical illumination. The difference between emotion in magical art and emotion in daily life is twofold: intensity and direction.

The intensity of emotion in magic is controlled, it is routed in specific defined directions. In everyday life emotions form a vague polychromatic wash that surges through the daily routine with occasional high points from personal sexual love, negative reactions to adversity or opposition, and manipulation by exterior agencies such as entertainment, politics, television and sport. Intensity of emotion as employed in magic does not mean imbalance or ecstasy; the word emotion simply means movement towards or away from an image within the consciousness. This image may correspond more or less to a physical object or person, or it may be idealised positively or negatively with no immediate outer corresponding object. If such emotions are not clearly attuned, they will move towards any manifestation (person, state or object) which holds an affinity for them, be it positive or negative. This simple law, rediscovered by modern psychology but always well known and clearly stated in magical techniques, is the basis of the much-maligned theory of 'sympathetic magic'.

In magical work consciousness is moved (emotion) towards goals which lie in directions normally ignored or unknown in daily habitual living patterns. There is nothing more than that to the use of emotions in magical art.

Religions worldwide employ quite extreme surges of emotion, both positive and negative, to control the energies of the mass faithful on a congregational or even international level. We can find this technique used extensively in the political religions of the west throughout our history to the present day. Magical images are not employed in this manner as the direction of the emotions aroused is inward seeking, moving towards the roots of consciousness, the ground of foundation of being, rather than the stimulation of destructive or impulsive reactions.

But magical work eventually percolates out through the individual magician or group; it percolates into the common imagination of the society or culture. Many areas of serious concern that occupied the attention of magical groups during the earlier part of this century are now the property of the general imagination and of public debate. These include the sanctity of the land, which has become the political environmental issue; sexual polarity and interaction free of stereotypes, which has become the issue of sexual liberation and equality; freedom from the slavery of inessential labour merely to survive, which has manifested as a new technology still in its most painful social stages of development.

More recently magicians have become concerned with the cycle of unjustified destructive energy, often symbolised by the fall of Atlantis in the mythical yet real past. This manifests as our irresponsible use of nuclear energy, not only in the context of weapons, but as a source of electricity; the magical research and concern which once appeared as innerworld communications and obscure papers has now percolated through into a widespread revulsion and opposition to abuse of nuclear technology.

When emotions employed in magical ritual reform, and return to an outer focus or location, they may move in a number of differing directions. It is at this last stage of re-manifestation that we must be very aware of the laws of polarity and balance.

The ethic of compassion subsumes personal emotion in the initiate; the response required is to be actively compassionate in both physical work and emotional direction towards outer objects and persons.

Many people who begin upon the magical path suddenly find it to be opposed or in conflict with their daily employment; fruitless activity to 'make a living' is suddenly spotlighted by the intense reversal of values that occurs in the early stages of initiation. In some cases the conscience activated by magical ritual and meditation will declare certain activities to be contrary to magical ethics; similar problems can arise with personal relationships. In this last area of definition many of the subtle powerful effects of magic first manifest themselves.

There are systems of magical art, which are touched upon in other chapters, which deal specifically with sexual polarities between our

106

physical human bodies; most of us cannot live up to the severe demands of such systems in the modern world, for they derive from ancient and less complex cultures in which sexuality, the land and human reproduction were holistically attuned to spiritual cycles of awareness and incarnation.

One of the crude rules-of-thumb developed in modern magic, particularly in the context of emotions, is that such powerful ancient techniques must be employed in a manner which renders them safe for modern society, but does not cancel their potency and effectiveness. The essence of this rule is that it is not advisable to manifest a magical image (god, goddess or hero) through a living person without the means of withdrawal from the identification. Such means are found within ritual technique, and this law is not merely a colourful re-statement of the psychological terminology of 'archetypes' or 'projection'.

True divinity, the origin of Being, may shine within us all, but god and goddess forms and heroic or tragic archetypes are not encouraged in magical art unless they are very specifically applied and subsequently de-manifested back to levels where the form or image or cyclical pattern is reabsorbed into the general flow of life energy. Such images are called up in ritual work, they are potent and highly energised, they arouse intensely emotional reactions in the magician or group; but they are not carried through into outer life in their primal forms. They are, however, available as expressions through a series of transformations which enable us to handle their potency with a degree of safety. Many of the techniques of magic are designed to act as filters or circuits for such energies to make smooth transitions from level to level. As with all such techniques, practice is required to develop style and efficiency, and it is in this context that meditation upon control of emotion (rather than emotion riding willy-nilly through the psychic reactions) is developed.

This concept is best demonstrated by an example. During a ritual invocation of the Goddess, men often feel irrational surges of fear, intense urges to weep, or similar emotions which may seem superficially to be 'weak' or even unconnected to the ritual symbolism itself. Such feelings are not merely the product of group interaction or psychodrama, as they might be in a sociological or psychological encounter setting. They are the ancient and hallowed responses to the presence of a form of consciousness which transcends humanity.

Whereas psychological or therapeutic techniques may encourage outer expression of this emotional response (say in the context of counselling upon problems connected to sexual relationships, which are the material-biological manifestation of goddess power) magical arts require the initiate to direct the emotion very specifically. There are several possible directions, which are indicated by Paths upon the Tree of Life, by the Tarot images, by traditional magical training.

The emotion aroused in our example may be offered up to the Goddess as a gift; this is the religious way, and is still featured strongly in Roman Catholicism. It has an important role to play in mystical illumination, for emotion offered in this manner is transformed by the very act of offering into love; fear literally becomes love through this alchemical process. In specific magical rites, a chosen image or expression of the Goddess may take the fear, turn it into a different energy, and return it to the magician. Such exchanges are made on a very advanced level of magic between male and female ritual officers (regardless of the type of emotion), but caution is usually advised in general work as this can cause irrelevant emotional fixations if it is not controlled properly.

Another way of describing the magical employment of emotion is to define the feeling as an energy; this energy not only originates in the psyche, but has corresponding effects upon the subtle energy centres of the body. If the energy is aroused through response to a magical image (as in the ancient awe of the Goddess referred to above), it may be moved upwards to a higher centre, by which process it is transmuted to a different mode. This is not identical to offering the emotion to divinity, but is the human psychic-biological reflection of such an offering. Ideally the two cycles of exchange are fused together as one... ultimately they are identical.

Emotions such as joy, fear, love, sorrow, longing, may all be ridden by the consciousness, employing them as sources of power to project the awareness into other dimensions. The practice of intense guided visualisation employs our energies in this manner, but it also employs many other forces which are not polarised as emotions.

We should note that the magician rides the emotion, and not vice versa; certain types of primitive magic employ emotionally generated trances or furore, but this type of activity plays no part in magical arts as they are developed today. If we revert to such practices, and many examples of such reversion are found in evangelist, charismatic or Pentecostal cults, we are turning our magical evolution of technique and art back in time. The obvious disadvantage of such entrancements and overpowering emotional storms is that they give so little back to the world; they are merely a trip for the participants, though probably less dangerous than the use of LSD.

In ancient cultures, specific orders of priests and priestesses were

108

reserved for such emotional furore; they were part of overall magical religious and philosophical practices. In social use today such trances and storms are utterly out of context...there is no ethical, philosophical or metaphysical overview in which they may play a useful role; they are atavistic.

THE GODDESS: ARCHETYPE OR STEREOTYPE?

It is at this level of the Tree of Life, Sphere Seven, that the magical or divine image has become overlaid with a stereotype which commenced with the substitution of a male for Severity at Sphere Five. This removal of the correct feminine image for Severity or Taking results in imbalance of the image of the sexual emotional goddess form; she becomes a simpering stereotype rather than a being of potency and Victory.

RESTORING IMBALANCE

During the twentieth and twenty-first centuries, the correction of our collective image of Venus is one of the most important magical acts; simultaneously we must restore other imbalanced images to their correct functioning role.

If, for example, a ritual group is formed in which members live up to sexual stereotypes (the strong manly male, the weak submissive female and so on) such a group will not be able to progress beyond the levels of the seventh or eighth Sphere (Honour and Victory, Hermes and Venus) as the imbalanced images of sexuality re-route our energies back to the outer world. The correct images, however, lead to inner liberation, and this is the *Victory* which must be associated with Venus.

While descending the Tree of Life, divine energy flows towards the Foundation and the Kingdom through a goddess form (to our imagination) which invites emotional response and sexual union... this power stimulates male or female regardless of physical gender, though in women it is polarised towards the male lunar image rather than the female Venus or Luna as a general rule. In magical art, however, the attention and flow of energies is reversed; Venus or the goddess form of the seventh Sphere reacts with our consciousness/ energy to admit us to higher worlds or dimensions. This is why emotional love can be either a hindrance or a great blessing upon the spiritual path; while the energy remains constant, its *direction* and fusion with other energies (shown by the Paths that connect the spheres) are crucial to our inner growth.

13 INTELLECT AND MAGICAL SCIENCE

The history of western culture during the last five centuries is defined by the development of the intellect, of rational thought, and, of course, of material science. It may seem from many of the suggestions and methods discussed in earlier chapters that logical intellectual processes, the skills of the mind, are not relevant to magical art. Such is not the case; the intellect forms an important part of magical science, but it must be kept in a proper relationship to our other modes of consciousness, most of which have been ignored by western culture or even perverted.

The intellect is the messenger and servant of consciousness, not the master. It forms only one tenth part of our potential awareness in the ancient systems of inner growth and initiation. Here is where the Tree of Life, even in its westernised forms, is a useful symbolic map; it shows an ordered pattern of relationships which the intellect may grasp; it is a map of the universe and of the universe within human awareness.

Upon the Tree, the properties of mind (intellect) are placed in the lowest Triad, the eighth Sphere (Glory or Honour). The classical god form is Mercury or Hermes, the messenger of the gods; an important body of magical science has acquired the name 'Hermetic' as its label, through associations in early literature with the god Hermes and the mysterious master Hermes Trismegistos, or thrice-great.

Enormous effort has been spent in developing increasingly complex mathematical and philosophical variants of alchemy, Kabbalah and other metaphysical sciences; yet this approach to inner disciplines is imbalanced without other qualities and experiences of specific consciousness. These qualities or modes are shown upon the Tree of Life; emotion balances intellect (Victory and Glory, or Venus and Mercury); both spheres are founded upon a biological matrix (Foundation or Lunar sphere) while all three of the lower Triad derive from sphere six, the spiritual centre (Harmony, beauty, or the solar world). (See Figure 7.)

A great deal of the more intellectual writing upon theosophy, the Mysteries, alchemy and other artistic sciences of consciousness is little more than a demonstration of the authors' academic ability or clarity of thought. The essential experience of the central symbols as living transformative powers is generally absent in such publications. Many self-styled occultists spend years playing with diagrams, numbers and biographies of past sages and masters; more academic experts may become obsessed with such fascinating but essentially sterile backwaters.

Our obvious analogy in modern civilisation is that of the clever teenager playing obsessively with computer games; the level of skill is high, some educational potential is truly present, but the end product is essentially valueless, trivial and potentially degrading, regardless of the science, training, technology and development of equipment. Modern magical arts seek, generally but not exclusively, to liberate us from the potential tyranny of the intellect, even in its weakest aspects of regular focus upon conditioned life patterns. Indeed, if the intellect can be turned to prove to itself that conditioned life patterns are false, it becomes a useful tool towards liberation.

In earlier cultures analytical thought processes were an essential stimulant to collective development; they acted as a corrective to our ancestral tendency towards superstition or more specific devolved magical atavistic practices. This tendency was blatantly abused by the orthodox churches, and eventually the growing intellectual clarity of the group consciousness threw off the restrictions of religious propaganda. The result of this development of one sole aspect of consciousness at the expense of all others is seen clearly in our materialist and self-destructive culture. In other words, the intellect has passed its peak of usefulness and has become a tyrant. Like the tyrant male stereotypes in myth, it should be replaced by a new Child of Light.

The magician should not castrate the demon intellect or reason, but bring it under proper balanced control; we need critical logical research to merge with our inherent tendency towards emotional or even frenzied modes of consciousness, the wild prophetic alternative states of awareness found worldwide through atavistic magical work. We must progress beyond the intellect, carrying it with us, and not revert to collective consciousness which is represented by earlier stages of cultural history. In practice the initiate experiences many of these states, but under controlled conditions as part of early training.

This progression of consciousness (which must in no circumstances be confused with the materialist concept of evolution) is shown upon the Tree of Life; there are seven Spheres beyond the intellect, three of which are connected directly to it by Paths. As discussed in the chapter on Paths and Tarot images, a Sphere is less important in isolation than in relationship to other Spheres. Thus the intellect should be, but seldom is, linked *consciously* to the operations of the emotions, discipline, and the biological matrix of all life. Each of these connectives is symbolised by a Tarot image.

The intellect (Glory or Honour, god form Hermes) is linked to Severity (or purification, discipline, break-down, god form 'Mars' or more correctly a female purifying power). The modern magician needs energetic connections of this category, and experiences of Severity are the most important initiations. We live in an acquisitive culture rife with pollution; many of our attitudes reflect this pollution inwardly blocking our innate image-generating magical power. The greatest value of the intellect in magic is still its critical power of judgement or assessment.

Superstition is more widespread today than it was in the medieval period, for there is no longer an orthodox dictatorial religion to define directions for belief and practice in our reaching towards the mystery of life, or the unknown. There are two proven ways of disposing of the trivial nonsense of occult revivalism; the first is the operation of genuine magical power, which is often a profound shock to the self-styled medium, sensitive, teacher or occultist living on mere words and fraud. The second, more generally encountered, is the operation of mental clarity, the intellect as servant of consciousness.

Although we have followed modern practice in suggesting Hermes or Mercury as the image for this eighth Sphere of consciousness/ energy, there is a more traditional image for the western psyche; a female image.

The goddess *Minerva*, closely linked to *Athena* by her nature, and to the Celtic *Briggidda*, is found in classical sources, Roman Celtic inscriptions and temples, and in the Mysteries of Merlin, which represent the foundations of western magical and prophetic lore in literature[14].

While Mercury may be tricky and deceitful, Minerva lives up to the curious attribute of HONOUR which we draw from Kabbalistic sources. The intellect becomes demonic if it is dishonourable or dishonest; there is an ethical pattern to the Tree of Life as well as a magical pattern. Minerva is the goddess of cultural development; she is related to the ancient triple-formed Goddess of primal cultures. The evolution of Minerva from bloodthirsty warrior maiden to wise tutor of heroes is the evolution of human civilisation.

Her image is particularly important in modern magical art, for we should always seek to correct the sexual polarities upon the Tree of Life, which are long corrupted by male stereotypical imbalance. Severity and Honour are both *female* magical images and divine properties of consciousness.

14 SEXUAL ENERGIES AND THE LIFE OF THE WORLD

As western culture emerges painfully from its long period of grotesque sexual imbalance, imposed magically by orthodox religion, the question of magical art and sexual energies attracts constant attention. Before we consider such energies further, there are two areas of misconception or wilful delusion that need clarifying: 'sex-magic' and sexual energy.

'SEX-MAGIC'

There is no such thing as so-called 'sex-magic'. All magic is sexual, which means that it works through polarised exchanges of energy. Conversely we could say that any type of energy, such as electricity, is as sexual as the act of physical intercourse; it merely works in a different dimension.

Old-style occultists, who grew up in a sexually morbid culture, treated the relationship between human sexual energies and magic in two different ways; it is difficult for us to judge today which is the more preposterous and dangerous of the two. Sexual polarity patterns were either treated as great secrets that could only be passed on to favoured (male) adepts, or as something to be avoided at all costs, on pain of terrible results. Unfortunately these far-reaching imbalanced attitudes are still prevalent in many modern books, classes and personal teachings; on one level they reveal how easy it can be to claim magical knowledge without ever experiencing its results, while on a more pernicious level they spread confusion and ignorance wilfully among students.

Much of this junk tumbles down to its inevitable place in the popular press, supported by the frivolous or even perverted activities of those who use 'the occult' or 'witchcraft' as a framework for their personal lusts, ranging from mere excuses for sensual licence to rare cases of evil abuse of sexual energies. We must be clear from the outset that none of the above abuses have any valid connection with the art of magic, least of all with any enduring initiatory tradition. Our second area of misconception concerns the nature of sexual energy itself.

SEXUAL ENERGY

Sexual energies are in no way separated from other energies; they are life energies inherent in the manifestation of all life forms upon the planet, and in magical traditions they run through many worlds or dimensions. The outward direction of our energies creates our physical body, which is both individual and collective. But even this body is not confined to the consensual world that we share superficially; this is a major teaching in magic, and cannot be passed over or ignored by the developing magician.

The matter of *direction* is paramount, for it is the rate, intensity and direction of our life-energies that enables magic to work. This great truth has been taught in all religions and esoteric traditions for many centuries, but if we divorce it from its philosophical or metaphysical roots within the spiritual perception of reality, it may be open to childish or wilful abuse. Direction is perhaps best demonstrated by an obvious example.

In primitive cultures, as in modern, there are taboos upon physical congress or intercourse between human and animals. Such restrictions have their roots far back in the depths of human cultural development, but are based upon some simple laws of polarity and direction of energy; sexual potency in male or female humans should not be employed to wilfully lower the threshold of our awareness. When sexual energies are directed in patterns that lower our awareness, we not only suffer individual injury and imbalance on many levels of our entity, but we further coagulate and rigidify the laws that maintain the consensual world. Although we have used one of the most ancient sexual taboos as a starting point for the example, it applies also, in varying degrees, to sexual relationships between humans at any time.

Paradoxically a great deal of nature magic, and some very advanced magical practices, is directly concerned with the relationship between human and other orders of life such as plants, trees, animals, and ultimately the entity of the land and the planet in its entirety. Many of these magical polarised relationships of energy (sexual exchanges) extend into other worlds, but before the initiate can enter such worlds in full awareness he or she has all trivial concepts of personal sexuality transformed and routed in more healthy directions. The relationships or exchanges made in magic are undeniably sexual; polarised energies are exchanged, entities react with one another. But they are not sexual in the commonly-accepted illusory sense of personal sensual gratification, or of the basic breeding drive that perpetuates species.

Modern psychology has claimed that sexuality is at the root of all human behaviour, reaction or interaction; regrettably this great truth has been limited in our materialist culture to gender roles and interplay of sensual (organ-defined) gratifications, often on quite subtle social and psychic levels. While restating a potent wisdom teaching long known in the Mysteries and esoteric schools, psychology reduces it to terms that are essentially limiting or even degrading to human potential.

Magical psychology does not limit sexuality to gender-orientated interaction; ultimately it emphasises the balanced androgyny or total Being reflected through humankind. If the magician is able to redefine his or her conditioned attitudes to sexuality, many of the more absurd problems in magical training could be disposed of rapidly. This redefinition eventually becomes *redirection* of energies, at which stage true magical experience becomes possible.

Having briefly considered some of the major misconceptions, from which a host of very subtle pitfalls are derived, we can move on to a more traditional magical summary of life energies.

THE FOUNDATION OF LIFE

On the Tree of Life, the ninth Sphere is called the Foundation. It is the energetic Sphere which expresses life forms; all higher Spheres merge into it (see diagram of Tree of Life) or grow out of it, prior to physical expression in the material world or inner direction to other dimensions.

The Foundation is linked harmonically to the Moon, represented by ancient goddesses of life, death, fertility, and tides of all sorts, both inner and outer. More specifically, it is the source of glowing energy inherent in all that lives, particularly biological life forms. This energy, which is really a harmonic or mode of the total energy of Being, as are all of the Spheres, is the foundation of our sexual life. We may direct it through discipline of the imagination (not merely by so called will-power) to radiate outwards or inwards. These directions are sometimes defined as upwards (inwards) or downwards (outwards), though such terms should be more accurately reserved for very specific acts of more advanced magical control of energy. The directions are not a matter of intellectual or literal debate, but are anchors for the imagination to employ, to help it move the energies. The actual direction becomes irrelevant once the ability to change our energetic orientation is developed, for at this stage a whole new set of directions becomes apparent to the inner cognition.

A third imaginative direction is possible, in which we let the foundational energy radiate spherically from its true location, without pushing it in any arbitrary direction. This is what is done in meditation upon the Sphere in a pure conceptual form, and leads to an inner conservation of energy.

In our bodies, the Foundation corresponds to the genital organs; which merely means that the biological outlet or intake for such foundational energies has a physical expression. It also has other subtle modes and areas of exchange which do not necessarily involve use of the sexual organs; the connection of the ninth Sphere to our physical gender is the individual and collective manifestation of life perpetuating itself as life-forms.

GOD AND GODDESS FORMS

All Spheres upon the Middle Pillar or Spindle are bi-sexual; in human terms this means we may relate to either male, female or androgynous images in meditation, visualisation and ritual pattern making.

Luna or Diana, the Moon Goddess, is known through myth and legend; she governs animals, the sea, the blood, all tides of fluids and movements of cycles and spirals; all life that passes in and out of the outer world. She is the goddess of formation of life and death, and acts as the matrix for many of our most potent psycho-sexual and bio-electrical energies. Magic conducted with the Element of Water is usually related to the Goddess Luna or the Goddess of the West; in Gnostic terminology it is the Archangel Gabriel who announces the turning and flowing of tides. . .in this case cosmic tides as higher octaves of watery tides.

There is also a Moon God, a male image for the Foundational powers of the ninth Sphere. In magical art, males relate to goddess images, while females relate to god images. This is the opposite of

117

customary teaching in occult literature, in which members of a magical group mediate powers of their own sexual polarity.

Enough discussion of polarity and inner energies has been offered in our preceding pages to suggest that mono-sexuality in spiritual matters is extremely unhealthy, and may in extreme cases lead to individual or even cultural imbalance. This is blatantly clear in modern western culture. If we consider natural tendency, and the practices of the ancient religions, we find that for imaginative work (as in outer life) the psyche reacts strongly to the opposite sex; in the spiritual disciplines the reaction is not sensual, it raises the sensual orientation onto a higher level, and transforms it.

Thus men may relate very effectively to the Goddess, and women to the God. Teachings of this type of magic are still present in debased forms of sexual activity related to changes of consciousness; true Tantric art, however, is rare in the west as a result of our lamentable collective sexual imbalance. Interestingly, if rituals are enacted in which women invoke god images and men invoke goddess images, there is far less danger of projection or false identification between the human magicians; they have already transformed their sensuality into energy directed inwardly through their polar opposite imaginal form (the goddess for men and the god for women) thus there is less chance of personalisation of the images through fellow ritual officers.

Much of the foregoing will seem like heresy to old-school occultists who still flinch even at mediating images of their own sex, but determinedly claim sole access to divine power in mono-sexual form. In fairness, it must be admitted that polar image working, as described freely above, should be balanced with mediation of higher aspects of the spiritual self. Such aspects tend to manifest as male if your gender is male, or female if you are female. The difference lies in the qualities of *meditation* and *invocation*.

This essentially magical art is most important in the application and development of the ninth and seventh Spheres in group ritual, using their energies to project the collective consciousness towards new goals and higher levels of understanding.

The Foundation is the realm in which the physical collective world is foreknown; its forms are moulded and defined before expression, and dissolved after removal from outer manifestation. The much discussed 'astral plane' is merely a reflective image that is attuned somewhere between the Moon and Earth, or the Foundation and the Kingdom; hence in traditional terminology it is realm of spirits that may be either good or evil, for it contains all possible combinations of energy prior to manifestation as physical expres-

118

sion. At one time magical arts were very much concerned with this sub-lunar realm, particularly in the ancient mysteries of reincarnation and magical conception of children. The cultures that were upheld by such practices are long dead, and modern magic aims specifically for higher ends, not through any type of ethical elitism or superior evolution, but merely because the philosophy and religion that supported such ancient techniques is no longer valid today.

In initiation, both the Goddess Luna and the Flower Goddess or Venus are used specifically to liberate energies from our frozen and coagulated conditioned states. The discretion of such magical liberation should come from innerworld sources, rather than mere human whim, as many sexual and psychological imbalances are found in the Lunar realms.

In ritual work, therefore, we tend not to invoke solely in the name of the Goddess but also in the name of her Son, who acts as a redeeming or balancing factor for the potent energies unleashed. Before progressing to the material Kingdom and the Four Elements, we close this chapter with an invocation. The verse may be used in meditation, visualisation, or as an actual candle-lighting ritual. It is of ancient origin, though expressed in modern language, and is suitable for both pagan and Christian beliefs as it incorporates both.

Invocation of the Son of Light (ancient prayer)

IN THE NAME OF THE SON OF LIGHT
THE SON OF MARIA, (1)
KEYSTONE OF THE ARCH OF HEAVEN,
HE WHO JOINS AS ONE THE FORKS UPHOLDING OF
THE SKY. (2)

HIS THE RIGHT HAND, HIS THE LEFT HAND, (3)
HIS THE RAINBOW LETTERS ALL IN RICH
FERMENTED MILK:
WE WILL GO IN HIS NAME IN ALL SHAPES OF SHAPES
IN ALL COLOURS OF COLOURS
UPON THE PATH TO PEACE. (4)

IT IS THE SON OF LIGHT,
THE SON OF MARIA, SAYING:
'ASK IN MY NAME AND IT SHALL BE GIVEN UNTO
YOU

119

ENTER IN MY NAME AND YOU SHALL IN NO WISE
BE CAST OUT'   (5)

DO YOU SEE US HERE, O SON OF LIGHT?
SAYS THE SON OF LIGHT:
'I SEE'.   (6)

Note: as a ritual this verse works through six stages indicated by the
numbers placed beside the text.

1) A candle is lit (using a taper which remains lit).
2) The taper indicates the direction of Height.
3) Two further candles lit, as the Right and Left Hand Pillars.
These make a Gateway before the original flame.
4) The officers progress around the Circle visualising the energies
and Elements of each Quarter. They return to face the Quarter in
which the light was lit, or the centre if it is placed upon a central
alter.
5) The officer(s) invokes and visualises the solar image, the Son of
Light, as strongly as possible, seeking to build a real contact and
presence upon the inner and outer planes.
6) The Light is radiated to the outer world, or to all members of the
magical group if a further stage of the ritual is about to be
undertaken.

CLOSING is usually conducted by a *Hexagram* pattern which is
described in the following chapter on The Assembly of the World.

15 FOUR ELEMENTS, THE ASSEMBLY OF THE WORLD

We usually assume that ancient worldviews have been disproven, that their cosmologies are ignorant, invalid and irrelevant. So ingrained is this dismissive attitude that we fail to realise that the function of such worldviews was different from our own; they are not, in fact, models that are supposed to summarise or represent material research into the physical universe. The conceptual models of early cultures provided inclusive but open-ended systems upon which consciousness was founded. In other words they were systems derived from intuition and psychic interaction, in which the truths were poetic or spiritual truths rather than 'factual' ones.

The open or harmonic quality of magical worldviews cannot be ignored; modern researchers assume from evidence that our ancestors had rigid systematic attitudes, but this assumption derives from a modern intellect fastening upon systems which were not founded solely upon intellectual premises. The Elemental system which permeated culture worldwide for thousands of years was not, as is so often assumed, an attempt to fit all known phenomena into a straightjacket. Even the medieval period in Europe, in which the classical and pagan worldview was rigidified within the dogma of the political Church, could not entirely absorb the magical quality into suppressive conditioning.

Modern scholars tend to assume that historical context and practice is the only way of analysing enduring conceptual models, such as the Elemental system and its many ramifications from cosmology to music to alchemy to magic. The plain fact is that such systems must be *experienced* and not merely analysed, summarised, and edited for re-publication.

The hallmark of magical development is this; it operates through systems of restriction, of symbolic orders which condition the psyche. But these orders of symbols are very carefully selected, and paradoxically they lead to liberation from the system itself, project-ing consciousness into new states and new worlds. The Elemental system can only be truly appreciated if it is applied in this manner.

Within the superficial rigidity of magical systems there are turning points or gates which allow glimpses of other worlds, hints at the real nature of the exercises. Such practical conceptual training patterns change with the consciousness of the magician; they are not in-tended solely as inclusive maps to comfort our ignorance by fitting everything into all-embracing categories. Naturally such an organic transformation cannot be experienced by a reductionist or analytical scholarly application of intellect; just as a music critic can never reproduce the actual experience of the work or musical concept that he tries to dissect.

One of the most interesting examples of this paradoxical quality inherent in holistic worldviews is astrology. Modern astrology employs a disproven worldview, based upon an utterly inaccurate set of co-ordinates; nevertheless it gives coherent and often remarkable psychological and spiritual insights. We might say that astrology and similar systems are closer to the real world than many of our current factual systems; thus they resonate accurately with human aware-ness, and the fact that their *outer* systems are disproven does not render them in any way *inwardly* invalid.

There is no suggestion, by the way, that we should attempt to take such systems literally in the hope that this will generate magic; this would be a path of extreme folly and imbalance. The magician uses all systems practically, and usually does not bother agonising over their so-called 'reality'. Systems which do not work are gradually modified or discarded; but traditional magical arts employ well proven methods and symbolic systems that have endured for thousands of years.

In practical terms the magician has to walk a carefully balanced path between systematic obsession and vapid liberality. The first extreme is common to literary occultists, while the second is rife among 'new age' enthusiasts. A genuine magical tradition, however, may contain material that has been borrowed by either of the two extremes mentioned, but with a significant difference; it endures through specific innerworld contacts. If you undertake to work within a magical tradition and persist with the basic symbols such as the Elemental worldview, you eventually come into contact with genuine teachers of higher levels of the tradition.

In the west this tuitional response occurs when the individual has transformed his or her worldview sufficiently to interact with the innerworlds, schools and teachers. If the ancient systems were as rigid and merely contrived as we are often told, no such holistic further levels of consciousness would be possible. The lines of contact with inner traditions are ancient and very much alive; they extend our open-ended systems of worldview and transformation far into the potential future; they are not mere echoes of decayed cultural practices.

In western magic the basic cycle is represented by the Elements, the Seasons, and a system of connected qualities, energies and spiritual powers. There are many variants upon the basic pattern, and groups usually develop preferences. *There is no rigidly correct system;* but there are harmonically related and powerfully effective patterns.

WORKING WITH THE FOUR ELEMENTS

The Elements may be defined in a very simple manner: *they are relative states of consciousness/energy.*

We may recognise the Elements in countless ways, for their assembly and recombination is an infinite connection of cycles. Through magical art it is possible to intensify certain energies by focusing the awareness, and the intent, upon the relatively isolated Quarters of the Magical Circle. The key word here is 'relative' for the Elements do not exist in isolation or total separation; they are part of a cycle. The basic concept is shown repeatedly in the Wheel, Circle, or Sphere that is central to all magical technique.

A mere summary of attributes is valueless; to grasp the identity of the Elements and their associated powers, the student must work through a series of meditations, visualisations and invocations. This series may be planned individually, and the best way to commence upon it is to draw up a basic cycle of symbols and attributes for an organised work programme, taking one Quarter per day, and allowing further time for work with the concept of the Centre or Middle Pillar.

Such exercises are not merely training work for beginners; they persist through to the most advanced levels of magical practice, and are often an excellent corrective for magicians who have become lazy and complacent through over-familiarity with their personal niche within revival occultism.

Let us consider a simple assembly of the Elements, which combines invocation with visualisation. As with all magical work, each exercise begins with a willed stilling of energies, and a contemplative approach to inner Silence.

Air/East/Dawn/Spring/Life (Sword or Arrow)

1) Facing East, or a suitable direction chosen to be magically East, the magician lights a candle in that Quarter, and invokes with the following formula (which is suitable for pagan or Christian): IN THE NAME OF THE LIVING SON OF LIGHT LET THERE BE LIGHT IN ALL WAYS OF DARKNESS, LET THERE BE PEACE TO ALL SIGNS AND SHADOWS.

2) Facing East with open arms, the magician acknowledges the presence of the light symbolised by the candle flame: BLESSED BE THE LIGHT ARISING IN THE EAST, OPENING THE GATE OF DAWN.

3) Facing East, the magician uses the ancient crossing formula, in which a field of energy is defined theoretically around his or her body. This is done by indicating with the right hand the points shown below, and defining the personal energies at these extremes, linking them imaginatively with the transpersonal energies symbolised in the words:

IN THE NAME OF THE STAR FATHER	(top of forehead, Crown, Above)
THE EARTH MOTHER	(genitalia, Foundation, Below)
THE TRUE TAKER	(right shoulder, Severity, negative or catalytic limit of energy)
THE GREAT GIVER	(left shoulder, Mercy, positive or analytic limit of energy)
ONE BEING OF LIGHT	(Circle around points defined from left to right sweeping arm around)
AMEN	(CROWN/SEVERITY/FOUND-ATION/MERCY and back to CROWN)

(Traditionally AMEN is a long humming chant, resonating vibrantly. It is a power-tone used worldwide in various forms, and is not limited to Judaeo-Christian practice.)

The final Circle encloses or defines the Kingdom, which is the world assembled within the magician's awareness.

4) Facing East, the Magician sits to attune as follows. He recites the attributes of the Quarter which he has previously learned by heart. This recitation, which may be spoken or silent, attunes consciousness to the connectives for the Quarter. This preliminary sequence is

then *ascended* and *descended* thus: *Air, spring, arising, flight, arrow, sky, dawn, beginning, opening, life*...(the sequence is then repeated in reverse order; this *ascension* sequence may be added to if required but it should not become too bulky or time-consuming).

5) Remaining seated, the magician now visualises inner scenes, usually with closed eyes and steady breathing:

a) A dawn landscape, with clear light illuminating a mysterious land. As the dawn light increases so does the energy of both air and life within the magician.

b) A gate opens in the Eastern Quarter, through which energies of Air, Life, and spring-like qualities flow into the Circle with a fresh blowing wind.

c) A Guardian being for the Quarter appears following the wind; he or she may take several aspects.

i) In gnostic magic the Archangel Raphael.

ii) In Celtic traditions the nature god Cernunnos or the Flower Maiden his consort at Spring. Both of these images have deeper universal aspects that may also become apparent in meditation.

iii) In esoteric Christian traditions, the figure of the Saviour newly arisen from his Tomb, shining with light and life.

iv) Alternatively, a youthful partly seen figure, either male, female or transhuman. This figure glows with energy, and acts as an inspiration and guide to the magician.

6) From this visualised assembly of the East, the magician may progress to a meditation upon the higher spiritual qualities, which ultimately are found in wordless, signless contemplation upon the essence of LIFE.

7) The Sequence is then reversed through the stages, concluding with the extinguishing of the light, and a final Crossing and pause for Silence.

SOME GENERAL NOTES FOR PRACTICAL WORK

1) Using the guideline pattern shown for the Element of Air, and consulting the diagrams and our other chapters, the magician or student should carefully assembly a full Circle of attributes, writing out all Four Quarters, then working around the Circle with one at a time.

The written version of the attributes and the primal invocations should be discarded as soon as possible; it is essential that this type of material is learned and absorbed by heart, as working from written scripts is insufficient for magical key patterns. During more complex rituals, scripts are often employed, but even in such cases the majority of the magical work is unwritten and relies upon skill in the basics that are described above.

If you are in doubt about the parallels for each Quarter (i.e. what is the parallel image [iv] for the West), this may be found by *ascending* and *descending* as described, and then meditating upon the Western Element and Qualities shown in the diagrams. The image will arise within the imagination if you conduct this meditation rightly (see Figure 8).

2) Once a full Circle has been worked through, the student devotes one entire session to the concept of ABOVE; one to BELOW, and one to WITHIN. Once again, basic attributes should be written out by isolating the material from our diagrams and chapters, but the key material comes from personal effort and right meditation. The key concepts are really all that is required to start magic working; thereafter all is discipline, perseverance and hard work.

3) As we assemble a magical worldview, so do we dis-assemble our regular habitual worldview. This assembly and dis-assembly are our personal harmonic of creation and destruction, but they work through a dissolution and re-ordering of consciousness rather than through an actual breakdown and recreation. This second stage is found during the higher initiations, which are symbolised by the various magical experiences and images. The stilling of the flow of consciousness, the inward contemplation of Silence, is our most potent magical weapon; not a shred of magical art can be undertaken successfully without it. It is this act of intent towards Silence that begins and concludes all magical rituals or work, for this mode of consciousness/energy firstly dis-assembles our false worldview, then enables our energies to be realigned. In higher stages of magical perception, the intent of Silence attunes our innermost centre of consciousness to the infinite Being of which we are reflections.

4) The energies that arise through the techniques described are not merely imagined, though the imagination is one of the prime sources of release for the Elemental energies both within and without the body of the ritualist or meditator. Traditionally such energies are shaped through the use of *Signs* and *Chants*, with the added definition of body movements and positions. Signs, Chants and movements all demand separate studies in their own right, but at this stage the following notes are useful in the context of our basic Circle exercise.

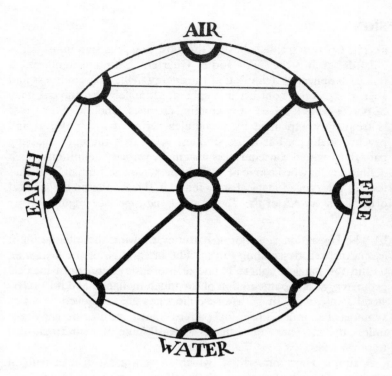

Figure 8. The Magical Circle.

Air: Beginning/Birth/Inception/First Breath/Dawn/Morning/Childhood/Sunrise/
Thinking/Questioning/Emerging/Arising/*Sword*/Arrow/Cutting/Flying/Moving
Liberty/Leaping/Exciting/*Life*/Wind/Fresh/Power/Sound/Spring/Germination/
Inspiration/Attention.
Vowel sound: E.

Fire: Increasing/Adulthood/Continuing/Exhalation/Noon/Brightness/Ability/Zenith/
Directing/Controlling/Incandescent/Burning/*Rod*/Ruling/Balancing/Upright/Seeing/
Relating/Harmonising/*Light*/Flame/Heat/Energy/Colour/Summer/Growth/
Illumination/Perception.
Vowel sound: I.

Water: Fulfilling/Maturity/Culminating/Second Breath/Evening/Ending/Fullness/
Sunset/Feeling/Receiving/Settling/Flowing/*Cup*/Giving/Purifying/Sustaining/
Nourishing/Cleansing/Clarifying/Emotion/*Love*/Autumn/Harvest/Sharing/Intuition.
Vowel sound: O.

*Earth:*Ceasing/Age/Rest/Exhalation/Night/Darkness/Peace/Starlight/Supporting/
Reflecting/Solidify/Manifesting/*Shield*/Mirror/Returning/Grace/Coldness/
Dryness/Containment/Touch/*Law*/Winter/Waiting/Preserving/Expression.
Vowel sound: A.

(Many more attributes may be added to these sequences; the four interactions listed
above are merely an indication of some of the major and traditional expressions of the
Four Elements.)

127

SIGNS

a) The Cross described above is the most universal sign in magic; as a flat design it is the Circle and its Quarters, but more significant is its use as spherical definition of the energy field. Consciousness and energy expand or contract in a sphere; ultimately the universe may be perceived as a sphere of interacting energies. The use of the Cross is frequently explained by a complex series of metaphysical and psychic analogies but in its simplest sense it is the encompassing pattern by which consciousness may make primary definitions. Such definitions may be cosmic or entirely personal and human; a further level of this type of magical art is found in the chapter on the magical orientation system of the *Tower and Landscape* (see Figure 9).

b) The Hexagram is a sign of harmony showing the integration of ascending and descending forces. The integration of the hexagram within the magical sphere is one of the basic exercises of magical geometry, as is the integration of the much maligned and misunderstood Pentagram. In both cases, the signs are employed to act as symbols of an inner conceptual pattern; they have no inherent virtue unless the magician understands at least some of their traditional implications.

A simple Hexagram ritual, which bears a great deal of fruit in meditation, might be expressed as follows (see Figure 10).

1) After a period of Silence, the magician lights a candle. This flame is visualised as the original Light of all being, shining through into the outer world by the intent of the magician, but also by its inherent nature as a flame within the field of Being.

2) Making a downward-pointing Triangle sign over the flame, the magician utters 'BLESSED BE THE LIGHT THAT COMES AMONG US', while inwardly invoking the power of spiritual Light in whatever form he or she acknowledges.

3) Making an upward-pointing Triangle sign, merging with the downward sign to create a Hexagram, he or she utters 'BLESSED BE THE LIGHT THAT LIVES WITHIN US', while inwardly attuning to the inner light or seed of Being within the heart.

4) Making a circle sign around the Hexagram, the magician utters 'BLESSED IS OUR BEING ONE IN LIGHT', and sits to meditate on the harmonious union of the inner light and the universal light.

5) This meditation is concluded by making the Sign briefly again over the flame, and extinguishing it. A period of intended Silence completes the working.

128

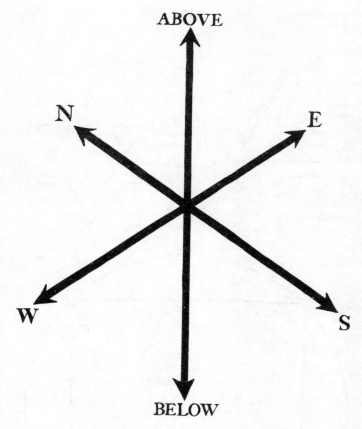

Figure 9. The Six Directions.

Effects of Signs

The simple ritual and meditation described above would be nothing more than a piece of gentle therapy if it was limited solely to a game for calming the random consciousness. There is much more to the magical Sign, however, than its human psychic application. Such signs are said traditionally to resonate through all worlds; they are universal symbols of the totality of Being.

This transcendent power of Signs soon makes itself apparent in magical work; the ritual described above may be employed to attune and balance a physical space, making the Hexagram in each Quarter. Through repeated workings of this type, a resonant field of energy is built up which is semi-independent of the magical operator. Certain

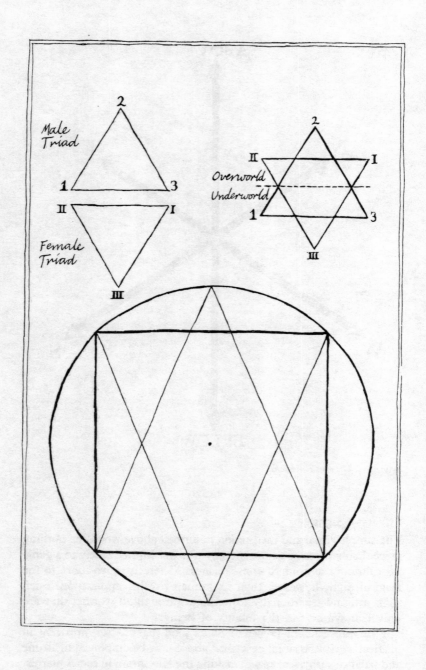

Figure 10. The Hexagram.

130

powerful sites in nature may be realigned or temporarily opened by the use of Sign rituals; the entire matter is a very precise artistic science which has hardly been touched on by revival magicians and theorists. It is from a garbled misunderstanding of this science that the dreary non sense about sign-making pentagram-waving occultists has been derived. A Sign will not *compel* anything or anyone; when it is used as a mere cypher or empty waving of hands, the power is not routed through the operator, thus the Sign does little or nothing.

The use of signs in modern magic should be limited to those which are clearly understood; playing with curious old sigils, signs, emblems or signatures plays no part in genuine transformative magic. Such relics from earlier cultures are the merest floorsweepings from a great temple science, handed down to us in corrupt form. Unless we are able to operate a small vocabulary of basic Signs, the complex sigils and squiggles are merely distractions. Having said that caution needs to be exercised, it must also be added that it is possible for the magician to develop signs and alphabets through a number of methods, and that such techniques sometimes form part of innerworld tuition. In all cases the material itself must be proven, valid and effective; if it is mysterious without any true connection to a generic magical system, it is usually rubbish. We should also add that a magician who is practised in the use of primary symbols may draw magical systems from hitherto unknown or obscure signs, but such transitions do not occur without a long training and experience.

CHANTS

Controlled natural breathing and simple chanting or resonant humming are techniques found worldwide in magic and meditation. There are also a number of very specific sciences of breath-control, which are not relevant to our present study of magical art, but which should be considered in the later stages of development. As a general rule, deep natural rhythmic breathing (always through the nose, never through the mouth) is the main requirement of western magic and meditation. Breathing exercises for general health are always beneficial to the levels of energy, regardless of an individual's practice of magic.

Chanting and resonating or humming help to aid concentration, to direct the flow of attention, and to locate energies within the entity. They may also be used to shape or define Elemental energies within the Circle, and a great deal of spurious rubbish has been published regarding this last application. There are no ancient calls from forgotten languages (such as the much-maligned Enochian of the magus Doctor Dee) that will work independently of the magician, just as there is no quick easy way to magical maturity and power.

In fact, almost any type of recitation, chant, call or resonance will work in magic, but there are a number of traditional systems which relate music to the Elements, and these are useful. The secret of all use of vocal utterance in magic lies in the discarding of unnecessary mystification; clear simple tones are an echo of the utter clarity of the voice of Being. Traditionally the universe was made from the Breath of Being breathing out a divine Word or Name or Tone...this originative Tone still resonates today through all utterances or energies. If we further mystify and confuse our understanding of this concept, we move away from the supernatural clarity of that Tone[15].

REASSEMBLING THE WORLD

Before leaving this basic method of attuning the Elemental Circle, some further developments can be briefly described. The circular or spiralling quality, epitomised in our world by the Seasons and the human life cycle, is merely one expression of the universal flow of energy. For most magicians, particularly in a modern social context, a genuine interaction with this cycle brings deep rooted realisations, changes of worldview, and an integration of personal elemental energies. But the Wheel is not the only pattern found in magic, and in later developments means are developed whereby the circular or spiral motion is completely obviated by a magical act that cuts across all established patterns.

In terms of magical training this may be summarised as follows:

1) Awareness and attuning to the Circle or Wheel of Life.
2) Amplification of this spiral pattern through transformations of awareness and relationship to Elemental energies and innerworld beings.
3) Application of a pattern which cuts across the spiral pattern of energy as a ground or field, for a magical transformation which suspends further cycles of the Wheel utterly. This application may be individual, group, or even universal in its degree. If it is carried out correctly, the operator is translated to another world. This tradition of physical translation runs through all western mystical and magical teaching, and is not to be taken lightly as curious symbolism.

132

16 MAGICAL ORIENTATION

Throughout our general discussion we have defined magical orientation within a) a Circle, and b) a Sphere. In training the student begins with the Circle, used as a flat plan upon the ground or floor, but almost immediately learns to extend this field of work through meditation and visualisation. It becomes a spherical field of energy; the aim of magic is to unify the individual and collective fields with the Universal Field. There are many interim stages, however, before this transformation is realised.

Our customary elegant maps, found in magical literature and tuition through the centuries, are supplemented in practice by a series of visionary exercises. Models such as the Tree of Life and Wheel or Circle define harmonic connections between the individual, nature, the solar system and the universe. But the danger of such maps is that we have a tendency to remain fixed upon their intellectual, mathematical or systematic levels; the human consciousness needs deeper and more comprehensive sustenance. The similarity is directly paralleled in normal life; we may study geography by detailed analysis of maps, textbooks, photographs, even films, but none of these can substitute for the experience of a real place. To reach the real places of magic, we combine the conceptual models or maps with certain rituals and pattern-making visualisations; these methods have been proved and hallowed through continual use, and their form has changed surprisingly little over very long periods of historical time.

The visionary exercises were originally taught by direct personal tuition; in some genuine magical traditions this method still persists, but it is rare in western culture today. The visions handed down by tradition may be used in imaginative meditation and visualisation, but they are also applied directly in ritual pattern making or ceremony where the idealised map of the Circle set out in a physical location is unified with the inner vision of a Sphere through the mediation of the human magician or group. The key to our early myths of humankind as gardeners, attuning the idealised earth to a divine plan, is found in this magical method.

The fusion method, in which vision and pattern-generation are merged together, is a powerful and significant type of magic leading to direct perception of other worlds. It is not limited to inner vision alone, nor is it a matter of individual spiritual meditation, though this features strongly in certain phases of the work. Magical fusion, of pattern and vision, may be undertaken by the individual or by a group; on a group level it is one of the methods by which innerworlds are defined and maintained.

One of the best visionary models in western magic is that of the *Tower and Landscape*. The historical origins of this construct are unknown, but as a magical tradition it is very ancient indeed, reaching back to early cultures predating our normal survey of history. It is still actively used today, and may be found in many forms. The Landscape and Tower form a central unit in the Mysteries of Merlin, which we know from medieval texts containing Celtic and pagan classical lore mixed with a pan-cultural cosmology upheld in an edited form by the Church. But it is not limited to references to Merlin, as it extends through many magical vocabularies or personae. The vision has a direct manifestation in the orientation of churches, particularly the great Abbeys which were often located upon ancient sacred sites. It begins upon the planet Earth, but culminates in the stars; traditionally magicians are taught that all temples, sacred sites, churches and locations of power are built upon systems represented by this vision of the Tower and Landscape. Once again, it must be stressed, we are deliberately making the *abstract* system, which is one of metaphysical orient-ation, into a *concrete* vision. Actual expressions in the outer world are still present for us to see in the form of buildings or of sacred locations.

Repeated work with this sequence of images, energies and directions will produce coherent results; it has been proven by generations of magicians and has the power of both enduring tradition and inherent psychic resonance. The sequence works for modern people just as effectively as it did for our ancestors. Firstly we shall describe the basic vision and its fusion with ritual movement and practice, then we will consider some specific developments that are found in practical work. The reader should refer to Figures 5, 6, 8, 9, 10 and 11.

THE TOWER AND LANDSCAPE VISION (Part One)

A Key to Magical Orientation and to Other Worlds

1) The magician sits in silent meditation, stilling the flow of awareness, approaching the Originative source of Being. This preparatory meditation is essential for all magical work.

2) The Circle is defined and opened, lighting a candle for each Quarter. The magician sits to visualise.

3) A strong Tower is visualised, to which the magician holds the Key. He stands (physically) and enters the door to the Tower, which is located (magically) in the East of the Circle. (This may be represented by physical Pillars if required.) Once within the Tower, it becomes the location of the Circle.

The magician climbs a flight of stairs (imaginatively) by spiralling round in sunwise direction, East/South/West/North (physically). This rotation around the physical Circle is made at least three times while visualising the ascent of the spiral stairs; at each Quarter the attributes of the direction, be it East, South, West or North, are *elevated* from Elemental levels through to Spiritual potencies.

The effect of this circling and elevation combined with visualisation is a raising of both consciousness and vital energies.

4) At the top of the spiral stair, the magician enters a circular chamber. (This is a higher dimension of the Circle already defined in the physical space.) Standing upright in the centre of the Circle, the magician looks East; here is an open door revealing a balcony and a dawn-lit landscape.

Turning to the South he experiences a door opening onto a balcony facing a bright noonday landscape.

Turning West he experiences a door opening onto a balcony facing sunset over the sea.

Turning North he experiences a door opening onto a balcony looking over a night landscape; the sky is filled with bright stars.

Looking upwards the magician sees a pattern carved upon the ceiling of the chamber. (This pattern will vary; it is seen with the inner vision, and should be noted and meditated upon carefully. Under certain conditions, the pattern may dissolve into a further level of vision.)

Looking down towards his feet, the magician sees a Fourfold Map of the World and its Elements, Seasons and Powers. He acknowledges that the Tower which upholds him has its Foundation within this circular pattern of rotation; he knows that in the outer world it is expressed in many different forms.

THE TOWER AND LANDSCAPE VISION (Part Two)

The Union of the Six Directions

1) The magician may now sit (physically) and contemplate any Gate at any chosen Quarter, or the upper or foundational directions above and below his central location.

Any specific visions, occurrences or contacts should be noted, either immediately, or more usually after the working has concluded. This magical experience is never outgrown, it persists for all of the magician's initiatory and transformative life.

2) The magician now reflects and meditates upon inner energies within his or her entity; they are a reflection of the energies of the universe or total Being.

3) The Four Elements, the Four Worlds or modes of energy, and the human Power Centres, are all unified through this meditation.

    a) The Elements are defined around the magician in a Sphere.

    b) The Worlds are defined as levels within that Sphere.

    c) The Power Centres are defined within the physical body.

Each of these three stages is energised by the imagination, but with practice becomes an actuality that arises rapidly while in the magical heightened consciousness.

The *Six Directions* of East, South, North, West, Above and, Below are attuned to the Quarters of the Circle, facing either East or one of the other chosen Directions. The Four Worlds of Origination, Creation, Formation and Expression are merged with the Power Centres of Head, Breast, Genitals and Feet (or Crown, Solar centre, Lunar centre and Earth centre). (See Figure 11).

Finally the Six Directions are visualised as merging into and emerging from a single locus; this is the root of Being, the seed within the individual entity; the centre of the magician *physically* which equates with the centre of the universe, or Being, *metaphysically*. This relationship is meditated upon while sitting.

4) The magician stills all energies, and enters into a meditation upon silence, the mystical state beyond Time, beyond Space, and beyond Energy. (He thus completes the cycle commenced with the meditation upon silence that opens Part One.)

THE TOWER AND LANDSCAPE VISION (Part Three)

The Return to the Outer World

1) The magician experiences consciously his or her breath as an aspect of the Breath of Being, which creates and uncreates, or

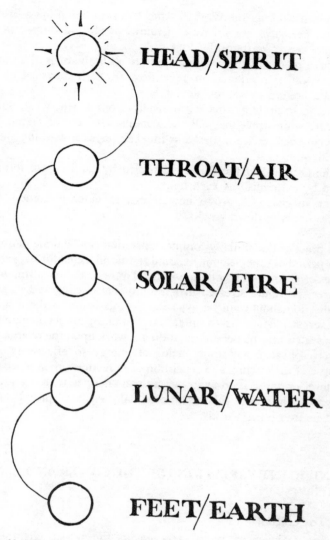

HEAD/SPIRIT

THROAT/AIR

SOLAR/FIRE

LUNAR/WATER

FEET/EARTH

Figure 11.   The Power Centres taught in Western Magic.
1) *Forehead:* spiritual illumination and transpersonal consciousness.
1a) *Throat:* the voice as a reflection of Being uttering itself across the Abyss of Time and Space.
2) *Heart:* solar central source of inner fire or creative energy.
3) *Genitals:* lunar central foundation of formative or sexual energy.
4) *Feet:* expressed body as a physical totality linked to the earth.
In magical arts these centres are gradually brought under conscious control and relationship through use of the imagination and ritual. They form a harmonious connection or holism shown upon the spindle or Middle Pillar of the Tree of Life (Star, Sun, Moon, Earth).

breathes in and out the Worlds. After this meditation upon Breath, the *Six Directions* are briefly re-acknowledged, and unified in the spiritual centre of the individual.

   (These phases of the working apply to all individuals in a group, who repeat the orientation regardless of their physical sitting position around or within the Circle.)

2) A reverse circling is made (physically) from North, West, South, to East, while (imaginatively) descending the Tower stairs. The magician emerges from the Door into the physical working area of the Circle.

3) The Quarters of the Circle (identified by candles) are formally closed by extinguishing each light.

4) The magician or group now return to outer awareness, and discuss or write down results.

With practice this initially complex operation can be done in quite a short period of time, leaving maximum time allocated for the various phases of vision and meditation in the Tower as the most important features. It should stressed that the physical circling and its inner visualisation should not be bypassed, as this fusion is the magic of the exercise. Attempts to enter the Tower by direct imagination while seated may be possible, but do not work upon the relationship between physical and inner fields of energy so effectively. The purpose of the circling and repetition of Directions upon more than one level or spiral is to align our human energies with the greater energies of the world; this fusion eventually acts as a springboard to boost us into other worlds.

SIGNIFICANT VARIATIONS OF THE TOWER AND LAND-SCAPE VISION

The Tower Roof

1) The magician or group proceed to the upper chamber as described, and view the Four Doors to the East, South, West and North.

2) A further circling of the tower chamber is made (i.e. a second circling and invocation of the Quarters). The magician visualises a gradual rising towards the roof of the Tower during this cycle, in which the roof of the chamber dissolves, and the floor level transforms into the rooftop. During this transformation the view of the Quarters may remain constant with its archetypical divisions of

dawn, noon, evening and night, or it may of its own accord change to a further coherent view. At this stage it is important not to become involved in the opening out of the magical landscape as a mere spectator; you are on the roof for a specific purpose.

3) Upon the roof of the Tower an innerworld contact is waiting. This contact may take a number of forms; he or she guides the magician or group through a very well defined visionary experience (hence the advice against passive viewing of the transformed landscape in phase 2 above). The innerworld contact will bring the human magician out of the experience often directly back to the Chamber of Six Directions, with its windows, floor map and symbolic ceiling.

4) From the Chamber, reverse circling is made as described above, and the operator or group returns to the outer world. Notes are made of all levels of the experience. Symbols often flash across the inner vision during the emergence from altered states of consciousness; these should be noted or roughly drawn out for future reference.

Below the Tower

There are several variants of this operation, the differences often being found in methods of approach; generally a cavern or underground temple is found below the Tower.

1) The Chamber is entered as described above by the elevation of the Circle, ascending the spiral stairs.

2) In one Quarter, usually the North-East, the magician visualises a small door (hitherto unseen). This door opens freely onto a second staircase; the direction is spiralling sunwise (East, South, West, North) but it *descends*.

3) The descent is visualised slowly and carefully while circling, and it bypasses the usual point of exit without any contact whatsoever. The magician or group emerges in small underground chamber or cavern. Here he sits and meditates upon the presence of Earth power. This meditation is traditionally enhanced by an image of the Earth Mother.

4) The ascent is made by spiralling sunwise directly to the outer Circle. After a brief re-orientation, the Quarters are closed as usual.

The Abbey

The sequence and its variants may be successfully attuned to the pattern of a Cathedral or Abbey. This form is particularly useful for esoteric Christian practices, though it is not limited to branches of Christianity known through orthodox history. Indeed, working with an Abbey model, the Tower and Landscape vision leads to some dramatic insights into the magical nature of primal Christianity and its expression within the innerworlds. In our outer world, most physical Abbeys are orientated according to the Six Directions.

In the Abbey variant, innerworld contacts take the shape of orders of monastics (monks or nuns); the UnderWorld vision involves a Mystery hidden in the cathedral crypt; the rooftop experience may involved angelic or even archangelic cosmic vision. Alternatively the rooftop experience may be an encounter with the Abbot or Abbess, who reveals certain secrets about the Abbey itself.

Ancient Cultures

The pattern will also manifest and work successfully as a setting within an ancient culture or civilisation. Keypoints are as follows.
1) The Tower is a tower for star-watching.
2) The Chamber is ritual chamber used to synchronise earth energies and star-energies.
3) The Cavern contains a primal image of the Earth Mother.

Relationship and Interchange Between the Variations

During early experience of this type of magical exercise, students often report that variants dissolve into one another. This harmonic reaction is quite natural in visualisation, but should not be over-emphasised or encouraged. Once again, it must be stressed that the working magician is not a passive spectator of inner visions; the techniques described are not to be used as a form of glorified dream television. If we do so, the power is dissipated and the group or solo worker is in some danger of psychic imbalance.

If the magical vision changes context from one variant to another, or to an unknown variant, the customary response is to rotate the vision around the Circle (i.e. view each Quarter as in the primary variant of the Tower chamber) and to return to a base-line variant through physical circling combined with inner visualisation. Experienced workers may be able to make fairly rapid transitions in this manner; the key is the physical movement linked to the imaginative vision.

A Note about Notes

Unusual aspects of the Tower and Landscape Vision should be written out as fully as the detailed workings described above; the operator need not be too surprised by unusual appearances, and if in doubt can always harmonise them through the cycle or circling described in our base-line method. Any discordant or absurd intrusions will be dissolved by this method, and banished finally by a return to central Silence.

Note-taking is *essential* for this type of work; during early stages it can reach voluminous proportions. Some magicians become obsessed with their notes; if this occurs you may cure the problem by deliberately burning everything and starting again. As work progresses the volume of notes will decrease; the purpose of note-taking is as follows.

1) To identify coherent repeated contacts, symbols and visions.
2) To objectify inner responses to the magical rituals.
3) To separate valuable inner experiences from trivial ones.
4) To provide a long term diary of events that enables the magician to recapitulate his or her magical growth through key patterns. In many cases these keys are not apparent for years and only surface during a magical re-assessment of a phase of work.

In earlier cultures without general literacy, the system was one of oral tradition. The initiate learned many verses of magical poetry and teaching, and these were correlated with direct inner experience over a period of years. This method still applies in an attenuated form today, in which the correspondences of the Circle or Tree of Life are learned by heart before full experience of their inner power is attempted.

The modern mind is very weak indeed when it comes to memory; in magical work with altered states of consciousness, many of the inner experiences are forgotten or totally refused by the regular awareness conditioned to outer directions. Note-taking immediately after a magical working can help to fix material that would rapidly be rejected or hidden by everyday awareness. With practice the art of memorising and fusing the separate levels of awareness becomes a conscious skill rather than a literary abstraction.

We must always remember that it is not the notes themselves that are useful, for they are really valueless. The value lives in the action of relating one area of consciousness to another through a physical interface; in this case writing. As practical skill in magical art improves, the physical interface becomes increasingly unified; ultimately it is our entire entity, right through to the physical body.

141

17 TAROT AND VISUALISATION

Before working through the various patterns and exercises found in this chapter, I would strongly recommend that the reader has a full set of Tarot cards ready to hand. The images are not specified in the text, so the reader may use whatever pack he or she prefers; but I have generally taken the images from the pack designed by A.E. Waite, which combined the so-called traditional Tarot with attributes of early Renaissance packs. It is my personal belief, for which no proof can be supplied, that Waite was familiar with the *Vita Merlini* either from the sole translation available in his lifetime or from his own personal research and scholarship; there is a tendency for his cards to reflect some of the Celtic ambience of the images (Tarot images) described in the twelfth-century text of the *Vita*[16].

The illustrations that accompany the explanations of the harmonic cosmology/psychology of the Tarot are merely maps, or sections of the Tree of Life and the Wheel or Circle of the Elements. To fully appreciate the Tarot images, they should be laid out in the patterns and combinations suggested, and further used in meditation.

I am aware that this harmonic system is different from that used in general 'occult' publication, though variant forms have appeared in some books in the twentieth century. There is no suggestion that this magical holistic approach to the Tarot as an aid to meditation and visualisation can replace or outbid the systems already used by students or adepts of systems such as that published from Golden Dawn texts or the papers of other magical teaching orders. Indeed, anyone well trained in the better-known Tarot attributes and correspondences will find that work with this system is very rewarding and effective; yet due to its traditional simplicity it can be apprehended by the beginner with far greater ease than the better-known correspondences and Path attributes of Trumps upon the Tree of Life.

It must be emphasised that Tarot images work in relationship to one another, and that the customary modern method of intense visualisation upon single images (Trumps) should be supplemented by the exercises in polarity suggested in the following pages, in which the images balance one another, and are shown to be rotations or cycles within a holistic worldview.

THE TAROT IMAGES

The connection between Tarot cards, now so fashionable that they are sold in toy shops, and the western esoteric traditions, is persistent but very confused. The confusion and contradiction of the original purpose of the Tarot has reached ridiculous extremes; the trend to use Tarot images for trivial fortune-telling obscures a deeper value; this problem has frequently been commented upon by students of symbolism. In the current absurd craze for 'the occult' Tarot cards have developed an unsavoury reputation; many people make a living by claiming to read the future from the cards, while nervous groups or individuals project their own fears and insecurity upon the images...then shrilly denounce Tarot as diabolical. None of this has any but the most superficial connection with magical arts; the problems and absurdities are excellent examples of psychic symbols (the Tarot) cut adrift from their metaphysical framework of growth or place within a spiritual tradition.

Magic is a method of arranging awareness according to patterns; the basic patterns employed are those illustrated in our various diagrams. When the patterns have been drawn, not only in physical space and time but in the consciousness of the magician, the relatively clear space contained within them is deliberately enlivened with images. The Tarot are the remains of such a set of images reduced to a portable pack of cards employed as a training device. The fact that Tarot images are sometimes effective in transferring hints or analogies of the individual psyche thus seeming to foretell the future, is a property of magical art or metaphysics; like any paranormal set of symbols or any set of symbols of any kind, such as those employed in science, they are open to abuse[17].

If we are to treat the Tarot seriously, they should be employed in a way that links them harmoniously with the other symbols of western esoteric practices, and fortunately the cards still retain firm connections of this sort regardless of modern speculative abuse.

Opposing the trivial use of Tarot, we find an indigestible mass of heavily-learned speculation connecting the symbols to the Tree of

Life, pantheons, astrology and other systems. Magical orders such as the Golden Dawn and various offshoots generated stunningly complex systems of relationship based upon very free interpretation and westernisation of genuine Hebrew mysticism. This was amalgamated with the literary magical systems that developed in the occult revival in nineteenth-century France, in which the Tarot played an important role.

One certainty may be affirmed; Tarot symbols are connected to the diffuse western magical traditions. Rather than attempt to repeat existing literary analyses, or to wrench Tarot symbols into preconceived moulds, a modern reassessment should attempt to show how the basics of the Tarot images are related to the basics of western magic; anything beyond this fundamental level is likely to be irrelevant.

The act of magic, making a magical sphere or Circle, is a minor repetition of the origin of the universe; the human consciousness wilfully mirrors the metaphysical shapes which intuition generates to define Being. It is not in any way required of magical arts to 'prove' such systems, nor should they be taken on faith in the religious manner; magic asserts that if the systems are applied practically, through experience, then certain known transformations will take place within the consciousness of the magician. Words are insufficient for such a process, and a symbolic alphabet is employed as an aid. This alphabet consists of two main types of symbol; mathematical and cyclical geometric units, and imaginal forms which act as matrices for complex energies. The Tarot, as we shall discover, contains both of these types.

Tarot images are not historically known in the form of cards before the fourteenth century; from the fourteenth through to the eighteenth century they spread rapidly through Europe. Early packs included many symbols not found today; stellar, planetary, mythological, images of the Humours and other developments of the Elements, all appeared in various sets. The so-called traditional Tarot pack is a relatively late variant, greatly simplified. The general opinion among esoteric scholars is that this standard pack is the basic form of Tarot, but there is no historical proof of this whatsoever. Whatever the contents, Tarot were a symbolic alphabet of images used for education; this worked on at least two levels, for the exoteric use would have been as pictures to instill virtue or education in the young, while the esoteric level revealed deeper meanings within the images, particularly in specific combinations.

To grasp the reason for the rapid spread of Tarot and related image-packs, we must remember that they served, exoterically, a non-literate population. Esoterically, they employed images which transcended literacy. The outer aspect of Tarot, images for visual education, is not at all unusual; we employ visual aids increasingly through computers, thus creating a non-literate (or illiterate) generation. But the comparison between Tarot images and computer visual images stops dead at this outer temporary expression; computer images as teaching aids are chaotic and fragmented through intense specialisation, they do not have any coherent pattern behind them, or inner level of meaning. They are merely pictographs or ephemeral images upon a screen. In this sense it is interesting to observe that our culture relies heavily upon an output of such short-lived images, television and computer games and aids. Yet our ancestors maintained complex enduring image systems for many centuries, systems which are still valid within the creative imagination today.

TAROT IN THE *VITA MERLINI*

The Tarot images are best evaluated by looking at their connections to a clear magical system; such a system, involving the Worlds, the Elements, indications of the Tree of Life, and a number of specific Tarot Trumps, is found in the *Vita Merlini* set out in 1150 by Geoffrey of Monmouth. This is the fundamental system of western magic, yet the text was virtually unknown and untranslated until the late nineteenth and early twentieth centuries. Tradition has a long memory, and Geoffrey drew upon the same traditions when he wrote the *Vita* in the twelfth century as were employed by many later scholars, alchemists, metaphysicians and magicians.

The *Vita* is chosen in our present context as an anchoring point in time; it predates the literary fabrications of modern occultism, it predates the developments of alchemy and Renaissance theosophy; it acts as a turning point between the older entirely oral magical teaching traditions, and the later literary accumulations. It also gives us a historical date for Tarot images at least two centuries before the first known packs of cards including such images[18].

Before setting out the spatial/imaginal pattern into which the Tarot fit harmonically, that same pattern taught to Merlin by the bard Taliesin, we need to look briefly at the history of Tarot once again.

Fortune-telling may have been undertaken with the Tarot from their earliest appearance as cards, but this was not the main purpose of the pack; the Tarot were a portable book or alphabet of combinations of images and qualities. Such systems were beloved by medieval culture, and were particularly useful to non-literate people with active powers of memory and oral tradition. This educational aspect of Tarot was lost by the Victorian era, though various sets of novel cards were produced that echoed such a function.

Over-enthusiastic occultists declared many obscure sources for the Tarot, including the temple images of ancient Egypt which were being re-assessed in the nineteenth century. As Gypsies used Tarot cards, the reasoning ran, and as Gypsy is a corruption of the word Egyptian, then obviously the Tarot were preserved from ancient Egypt. Unfortunately for such glamour, the Gypsies were one of the last waves of Indo-European travellers from Northern India, and had no connection with Egypt. Like any itinerant group of people, they collected oral and visual traditions of the lands in which they travelled, adapting them into their own culture. Tarot were an ideal source of educational pictoral images with an esoteric or psychic content; they were used by the Gypsies because such packs were widespread throughout both eastern and western Europe from at least as early as the fourteenth century, with the images having some kind of currency (not defined as cards by historical examples, but likely as cards or pictures in addition to images in myths and legend) at least as early as the twelfth century.

The point of this short historical digression is not merely one of proof of an early date to Tarot; it demonstrates that people used Tarot images to generate specific reactions, either of basic education, story-telling, prediction, or, as we shall see soon, magic and cosmology. In other words, Tarot are not the hoary secret wisdom of hierarchical Egypt, nor are they diabolical emblems for unhallowed practices; they are the symbolic alphabet of western consciousness. Furthermore, many of the images are shared worldwide, as are the geometric and cosmological patterns inherent in the Tarot pack.

The presence of a number of Tarot Trumps and other aspects of Elemental cosmology in the twelfth-century *Vita Merlini* and the *Prophecies of Merlin* suggests that such images were drawn not only from classical sources known to the medieval scholars, but from Celtic tradition preserved through popular tales or songs. This tradition in turn derives from Druidic wisdom teachings, which persisted in various attentuated forms until well into historical times. The magical transformative connections are overt in the Merlin books, and the cosmology which they contain is basically that of western magic.

What must be stressed is that the system native to western magic is not generally published in modern occult literature; many of the isolated details of the genuine system are known, but the fusion, and the application of Tarot images in particular, is not. It is because of the confusion arising from modern occult literature that we have deliberately employed the *Vita Merlini* as an example, rather than merely state the traditional system baldly without its historical source.

How may we relate the Tarot images to the Wheel or Circle or Sphere and to the more complex polarity patterns of the Tree of Life? More important, how can we establish a relationship that actually works in magic and meditation, and is not merely a complex fabric of intellectual juggling? The answer is that such a relationship already exists; it is inherent in the magical arts, including the Tarot images which act as a map of the universe; both the universe within and the universe without.

Two types of symbolism must be examined and fused together; both are found in the Tarot pack, both are employed in magical work, and both are taught in the text of the *Vita Merlini*. They are as follows: *Paths* or connections upon the Tree of Life, and *Elements* or relative states of energy/consciousness around the magical circle. The *Paths* employ the major Tarot images, or Trumps, while the *Elements* are represented by the minor images or suits.

MINOR CARDS

As has been frequently described, the four suits are the origins of the modern playing card suits, and represent the Four Elements:

AIR/SWORDS; FIRE/WANDS; WATER/CUPS; EARTH/ SHIELDS.

Each suit of minor cards runs from Ace to Ten, and employs four People derived from combinations of Elemental attributes. They are an early system of psychological categorisation: PAGE/EARTH; KNIGHT/AIR; QUEEN/WATER; KING/FIRE. Thus each Person will have quite distinct qualities, deriving from the combination of the Elements he or she represents.

This simple system shows each Element manifesting through Ten Stages (Ace–Ten), suggesting the Tenfold Tree of Life and the Fourfold Elemental Cycle (of relative energy/consciousness) appearing in each Sphere of the Tree, or in the Tree as a whole entity. To this are added Four People for each Quarter; they experience the elemental-qualitative effects of the suits in action. The origins of this worldview are ancient, merged from classical philosophy and native western traditions such as Druidism or chthonic cult practices, with the broad spectrum of gnostic and Hermetic philosophy which incorporated the remains of older magical and metaphysical wisdom teachings.

As a series of pictoral images, the system may be employed for meditation, for story-telling, for education; it is a system of basic interactions. It is easy to see how it could be corrupted into crude fortune-telling, without knowledge of its deeper roots.

MAJOR TRUMPS

These images are of a different order of symbolism, less open to direct rule-of-thumb interpretation. They are frequently ascribed to the Paths that connect the Spheres of the Tree of Life; in this role they should act as a related set of images that enables a flow of consciousness between polarised states of opposites or complementaries.

The simplest way to find the relationships inherent in the Tarot, which are merely visual expressions of enduring magical images or forms that define forces encountered both inwardly and outwardly, is to discover their relationship to the pattern of Worlds. This relationship is organic or harmonic, and different in many respects to the correspondences normally associated with Tarot images in popular occultism.

In the *Vita Merlini*, Merlin in the role of first-and-last-man learns the universal pattern, and the reflections of that pattern upon earth, right through to human sexuality and the cycle of the seasons. He hears of orders of innerworld beings, and of mysterious realms under the earth where rejuvenation and transformation are found. Merlin also travels around the Wheel of Life, the seasons, with various adventures and people placed clearly at specific seasonal or transitional points upon the circular map. The similarity to the Tarot system is unmistakable, from the minor cards of the elements and interactions, through to the major cards embodying specific magical persons or images. It is possible to restore a harmonic pattern of Tarot images from the cosmology and magical psychology of the *Vita;* furthermore, although the mathematical Tree of Life does not appear in the Merlin texts, its cosmic equivalent (Worlds or planes of manifestation) is clearly described, giving us insights into the true

148

position of Tarot Trumps upon the Tree. The pattern may be summarised as follows, with the aid of the illustrations.

THE ELEMENTS, SPHERES AND WORLDS

The universe originates with a fourfold expression, four primary powers out of one central seed of Being. These are the abstracts or spiritual matrices which we experience as LIFE, LIGHT, LOVE, LAW, but which are also the Four Elements, AIR, FIRE, WATER, EARTH.

This fourfold pattern devolves through a series of states or Worlds, and the order is perceived by human intuition and observation, a fusion of the inner and outer worldviews. In the most simple summary possible, these states are: STAR WORLD, SUN WORLD, LUNAR WORLD, EARTH WORLD. In each of these four Worlds, the fourfold cycle of rotation or relativity appears both as manifest creation (Stars, Sun and planets, Moon, Earth) and as different orders of beings (Archangels, Angels, Spirits, Humans). The above is merely a simplification, a description of the basic harmonic pattern found in esoteric tradition; specific systems vary in detail and there is no suggestion that the basic pattern is 'correct' while various other forms are 'incorrect'.

The value of an uncluttered un-sectarian system is that we may employ it directly for visualisation and meditation without concern over technical details. One of the greatest weaknesses of modern esoteric studies is the intellectual nit-picking and squabbling over details; in living magical art the primary patterns are generated and harmonised and all else follows. This does not imply, of course, that accuracy, research and attention to detail must be abandoned; modern magicians are beginning to realise how specific the ancient traditions are; quaint confused literary occultism must be balanced with both detailed research and practical work. The intellectual assessments, however, are mere dross without the spiritual insight; this is exactly why a great deal of modern publication of magical, alchemical, occult and esoteric subjects is only journalism.

When we employ the pattern of Worlds and the cycle of Elements, we are on one hand regenerating humankind's primal intuitions regarding the universe, and on the other defining the basic patterns that lead to highly sophisticated solid geometry and mathematics.

The *Star World* consists of the stars, of the depths of space and its primal energies, and of beings and states of consciousness which

149

relate this stellar state. In orthodox religion and in the medieval magical systems such as the *Vita Merlini*, these beings are called archangels. In magical art they are experienced as highly energised modes, as beings, as transcendent awareness that flies beyond time and space.

The *Solar World* consists of our individual star, the Sun, and its attendant bodies. Traditionally this world is occupied by angels and planetary beings who sing and declare the power of Harmony through the dance of orbits and energies. In magical work, these states and beings are encountered imaginatively, but not fantastically, by the initiate as he or she develops and expands consciousness.

The *Lunar World* is intermediary between higher and lower modes of awareness; it consists of the Moon, and orders of semi-material beings who may (traditionally) be kindly or ill-disposed. This world corresponds to the biological consciousness of all life forms, and to the unconscious of modern psychology. It does not, however, correspond to the UnderWorld of magical psychology and cosmology, a world which we shall summarise shortly.

The *Earth World* is our planet occupied by humans and many life forms; it has four winds, four seas, four primary regions. This magical geography is not intended to be literal, but to act as a foundation for magical and meditational work in which the consciousness generates a harmonic or holistic worldview. Many ancient cultures built their cities and measured land divisions upon such cosmic or intuitional maps; they reflected the magical understanding of the universe upon the physical body of the planet. The scale of such undertakings varies from the most simple magical circle drawn outdoors with a staff, to vast structures and entire countries.

The Earth contains the Gates to the UnderWorld, which is found by passing through the most solid expression of Being, the material planet. The UnderWorld is a reflection of the universe, and initiatory techniques were employed by which inner transformation was catalysed through experiences in the UnderWorld rather than through the apparently vast pathways of the universe. The paradox is only solved by meditation or magical experience, and not by mere description.

Thus we have four Worlds or levels of manifestation, and an UnderWorld which reflects the totality by representing ultimate Being in finite matter. (Figure 12 shows the UnderWorld Tree of Life.)

This system is identical with the more modern publication of Kabbalistic worlds: Originative (star), Creative (solar), Formative

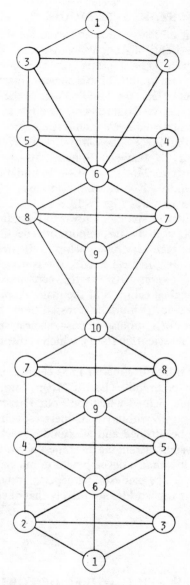

Figure 12. The UnderWorld Tree of Life.

(lunar) and Expressive (Earth). The Underworld reveals an inverted mirror-image Tree of the Universe, hidden within the earth, and inherent in the depths of human consciousness.

151

THE TRUMPS: STAR, SUN, MOON

If we take a pack of Tarot cards and examine the major images or Trumps in the light of the above pattern, certain cards are immediately relevant. The Trumps Star, Sun, Moon, and the Four Aces form the central Spindle of this ancient cosmology/psychology; these Trumps are, in fact, the Middle Pillar of the Tree of Life, with the Aces and the derivative numbers, through to Ten of each suit, representing the Fourfold cycle manifesting through ten stages (the Ten Spheres of the Tree). The natural position for the Trumps of Moon, Sun, Star, is between Spheres 10–9 or Kingdom and Foundation (Earth to Moon); 9–6 or Foundation and Harmony (Moon to Sun) and 6–1 or Harmony to Crown (Sun to Origin or Being). (See Tree of Life, Figure 13.)

This central pillar or spindle, Crown to Kingdom, Origination to Expression, Spirit to Body, has important reflections in the psyche, the body, and the planetary relationship to the heavenly patterns as seen from Earth. In practical magic, the concept is taken up and employed in the fusion between the consciousness/body of the magician, the imaginal compass of the magical sphere or circle, and the geocentric zodiac. It must be stressed here that the geocentric system is a system of symbols of consciousness analagous to stellar observation, and its scientific status, which is disproven, is only part of its value.

If we consider this entire matter in as clear a manner as possible, the Middle Pillar or Spindle (Earth, Moon, Sun, Stars) delineates areas of Above and Below, while the Four Directions or Elements give a psychic compass within which energies, concepts, images and experiences may be attuned and allocated. (See Figure 9.)

The magical system, arranging awareness according to patterns, is nothing more or less than a development of our natural unconscious growth through various modes of perception and orientation. But it extends through many worlds, not merely that of collective life upon the planet Earth.

JUDGEMENT, JUSTICE, WHEEL OF FORTUNE

Having discovered that the Trumps Sun, Moon, Star make the central spindle of the magical sphere, circle, or Tree of Life, we can make an immediate allocation of three further Trumps: Judgement, Justice, The Wheel of Fortune.

These three cards represent consciousness through the worlds;

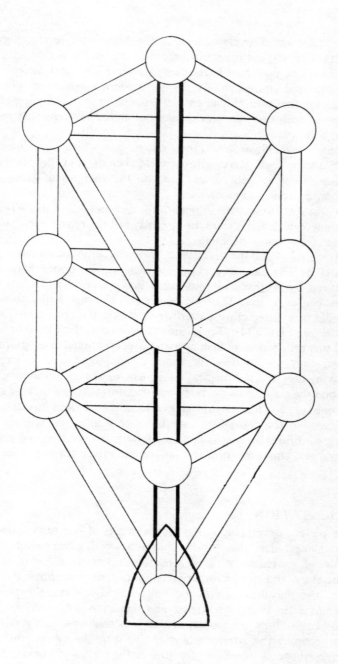

Figure 13. Star, Sun, Moon and the Spindle.

153

their function is encapsulated in the traditional terminology of mystical or magical texts. *Archangels* in the Stellar World have the transcendent power of Judgement, which is a perfect interplay of Wisdom and Understanding. In our modern magical parlance, we might say that transhuman entities balance an understanding of the universe with the power or wisdom of stellar patterns that merge time and space.

Angels in the Solar World mete out Justice, which is the interplay of Severity and Mercy. Innerworld beings and properties of consciousness apprehend and mediate the energies of giving and taking, analysis and catalysis.

Spirits and humans are subject to the rise and fall of the Wheel of Fortune, which arises from the interplay of Victory and Glory, or the cycle of the emotions/intellect.

As we transcend the first level of interplay, emotions/intellect, the Wheel of Fortune or cyclical interaction, the upper harmonics pictured by Justice and Judgement are perceived and come into more conscious use. Thus we have three Trumps which cross the spindle in a flat picture pattern, or encircle the sphere in a solid model (see Figure 14). When using these models there is no implication that they represent firm or spatially proportional or geographical areas; they are models for inner development and conceptual growth; they are the magical equivalent of the gymnasium which enables the training of the body and transforms it to a healthy state. No one suggests that a gymnasium *is* health; no serious magician will believe that the cosmologies are ultimate reality, but will act and work with them as interfaces between human awareness and greater awareness, whatever form that awareness may ultimately take.

ORIENTATION

The pattern developing is not only a means of psychic orientation linked to physical observation, but merges with advanced or higher modes of awareness; it shows a relationship between Earth, Moon, Sun, Stars, and carries important implications concerning the Pole Star, and the ultimate Galactic Pole. In magical art, the physical directions are attuned to stellar and metaphysical directions. The root of this entire conceptual system is both simple and profound, and occupied the attention of many early philosophers: the most perfect shape is a sphere, for this is the shape of consciousness expanding or contracting equally through inner or outer space.

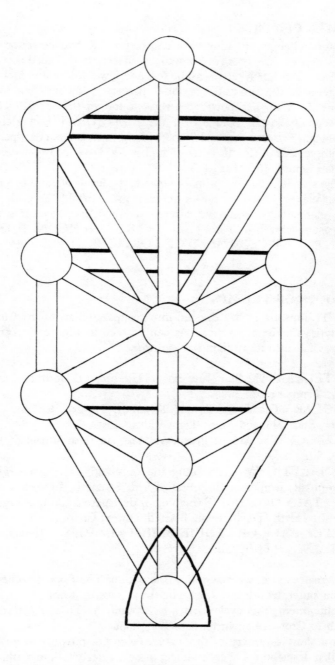

Figure 14. Judgement, Justice and the Wheel of Fortune.

POWER CENTRES

In human beings, the four worlds correspond to four power centres or nodes of life energy (sometimes inaccurately called psychic centres). The Earth relates to the feet and lower limbs; the Moon to the genitals; the Sun to the region of the heart; and the Stars to the forehead. A further power centre is found in the throat, which corresponds to the Bridge over the Abyss (DAATH in Hebrew Kabbalah) between Sun and Stars. This Abyss is interstellar space in the universe, but the rift between higher and lower consciousness in human beings. (See Figure 3.)

The spindle, the four primary powers, the levels of equilibrium in consciousness, the four power centres, the fourfold life cycle, the four elements, seasons and directions are defined by six simple images, preserved in Tarot cards: STAR, SUN, MOON, JUDGEMENT, JUSTICE, WHEEL OF FORTUNE.

GROUPS OF TRUMPS

The Trumps are in fact divided into groups: Stellar, Solar, Lunar, Analytic, Catalytic, Cyclical. As can be seen in Figure 15, certain images fall into more than one group.

1) STELLAR: The Star; Judgement; Hierophant; Hermit; Hanged Man; Temperance.
2) SOLAR: The Sun; Tower; Strength; Lovers; Chariot (also Moon; Star; Hanged Man; Temperance; Justice).
3) LUNAR: The Moon; Priestess; Magician (also Wheel of Fortune, Sun).
4) ANALYTIC IMAGES (outgoing or creative/giving energies): Hierophant; Emperor; Empress; World, Strength; Lovers.
5) CATALYTIC IMAGES (ingoing or destructive/taking energies): Hermit; Death; Devil; Fool; Blasted Tower; Chariot.
6) CYCLICAL OR EQUILIBRIUM IMAGES: Judgement; Justice; Wheel of Fortune.

In a greater cycle, we may follow the path of The Fool, who begins in the outer world and works his way inwards towards spiritual enlightenment; this cycle carries us around the Tree of Life from Earth to Crown, Crown back to Kingdom.

In a short summary of this nature, it is not possible to go into detailed descriptions of each image; these are dealt with in a number of reference works, some of which are given in the Bibliography.

156

POLARITY

The harmonic/spatial system of using Tarot images in magical visualisation depends upon polarity and relationship between the images. Each image is made from the relationship between two powers or Spheres as may be seen from our basic Tree of Life figures. Thus THE LOVERS is an image representing the polarisation between HARMONY or Beauty, the sixth Sphere or Solar Being, and VICTORY the seventh Sphere or power of Venus. When the emotions (Venus) and the central spiritual being (The Sun) are fused together in the consciousness of a human being, harmonious love is the result. But this fusion appears also on a collective and solar or angelic scale, if we follow the system of Worlds or levels through. Love is a power and not a sentiment, though it may be expressed as a sentiment in limited human terms.

MAGICAL TRAINING WITH TAROT TRUMPS

Each Trump or Path may be summarised in a few key words; one of the main magical training exercises is to make such a summary. The method is as follows.

1) Study the harmonic Tree of Life with its attributes and polarities for each of the Ten Spheres. (Figures 3, 13, 14 and 15.)
2) Lay out the Tarot images that correspond to each Path, as they show the interaction of each pair of Spheres.
3) Draw up a list of the key words for each Image (i.e. LOVERS/ SUN/VENUS/BEAUTY/HARMONY/VICTORY/CENTRALITY/ EMOTIONS). Meditate upon the image and attempt to fuse the qualities of the key words together. Working through all twenty-two images in this way is a long but rewarding cycle of meditation and visualisation. Using key words and the picture images is more productive than learning attributes from text books, as this method enlivens our imagination, and we generate a relationship between the images and the powers that they represent. To learn about such images by digesting lengthy verbal interpretations (the usual method offered in textbooks) is time-consuming and often distracts us from the root value of the Tarot, which should act as stimuli to the imaginative forces within us.
4) Draw up a list of polarised relationships between the Trumps. This stage cannot be fully developed until (3) above has been worked through, but early attempts at finding these relationships may still be rewarding. An example would be thus:

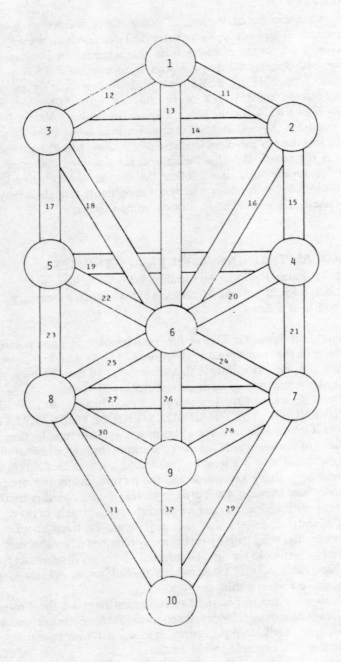

Figure 15.   Tarot Trumps upon the Tree of Life.

SPHERES

1) CROWN	SPIRIT	SOURCE OF ORIGINATION
2) WISDOM	OUTGOING UNIVERSAL POWER	STAR FATHER
3) UNDERSTANDING	INGOING UNIVERSAL POWER	DEEP MOTHER
4) MERCY	CREATIVE OUTGOING POWER	GREAT GIVER (MALE)
5) SEVERITY	DESTRUCTIVE INGOING POWER	TRUE TAKER (FEMALE)
6) HARMONY	BALANCING POWER OF CENTRALITY	SOURCE OF CREATION
7) VICTORY	EMOTIONS AND IMAGES	ATTRACTION
8) HONOUR	INTELLECT AND FORMS	DISSECTION
9) FOUNDATION	GENERATIVE POWER/ REFLECTION	SOURCE OF FORMATION
10) KINGDOM	FOCUS OF EXPRESSION	EARTH MOTHER

The Abyss separates Spheres 1/2/3 from the created solar system or universe, while Paths 13/15/16/17/18 bridge this separation.

PATHS

11) Fusion of Originating Spirit and Outgoing Power: THE HIEROPHANT.
12) Fusion of Originating Spirit and Understanding: THE HERMIT.
13) Fusion of Crown and Harmony: THE STAR.
14) Fusion of Wisdom and Understanding: JUDGEMENT.
15) Fusion of Outgoing Power and Compassion: EMPEROR.
16) Fusion of Harmony and Wisdom: TEMPERANCE.
17) Fusion of Severity and Understanding: DEATH (Cosmic Change).
18) Fusion of Understanding and Harmony: HANGED MAN.
19) Fusion of Severity and Mercy: JUSTICE (harmonic of JUDGEMENT).
20) Fusion of Mercy and Harmony: STRENGTH (harmonic of TEMPERANCE).
21) Fusion of Mercy and Victory: EMPRESS (polar harmonic of EMPEROR).
22) Fusion of Severity and Harmony: TOWER (harmonic of HANGED MAN).
23) Fusion of Severity and Honour: GUARDIAN (harmonic of DEATH) (mis-called 'Devil' in modern usage).
24) Fusion of Victory and Harmony: LOVERS (harmonic of STRENGTH).
25) Fusion of Honour and Harmony: CHARIOT (harmonic of TOWER).
26) Fusion of Harmony and Foundation: THE SUN (harmonic of THE STAR).
27) Fusion of Honour and Victory: WHEEL OF FORTUNE (harmonic of JUSTICE).
28) Fusion of Foundation and Victory: PRIESTESS (polarisation of LOVERS).
29) Fusion of Victory and Kingdom: THE WORLD (Harmonic of all outgoing Paths).
30) Fusion of Honour and Foundation: MAGUS OR PRIEST (polarisation of CHARIOT).
31) Fusion of Kingdom and Honour: THE FOOL (Commencement of all ingoing Paths).
32) Fusion of Foundation and Kingdom: THE MOON (Harmonic of THE SUN).

BLASTED TOWER: power of Beauty/Severity, breaking down in order to recycle energies/substance: the power of solar or harmonic destruction; necessary elimination and transformation. This is in a relationship with STRENGTH, the power of Beauty/Mercy, building up towards creative generation. Both Paths are centralised by the Sphere of Harmony or Beauty, one being the negative or severe pole, the other being the positive or merciful pole. Just as the Spheres have sexual or polarised relationships, so do the Paths (shown by Tarot Trumps) of interaction. (See Figure 16.)

In this context it should be suggested that the Paths are more valuable to the magician than the Spheres, although modern occultism tends to concentrate more upon the Spheres of the Tree of Life, as it often loses sight of the harmonic relationship of paths which we have suggested above and in our various illustrations. While we, as humans, may be able to appreciate intellectually the power of pure Severity or Taking (Sphere 5) and even enter into this conceptual realm through meditation, the *effect* of this magical exercise is likely to manifest through one of the Paths connected to that Sphere (Tower/Devil/Death/Justice). A Path defines the direction and interaction of the pure energies invoked in ritual; the sooner the magician understands the Paths, their Images and their effect, the sooner he or she grows up magically.

The fourfold exercise suggested above is an invaluable magical training programme, and will be useful even to experienced workers if they have not experimented with the ancient harmonic/cosmological system of Path relationship, shown in the Tarot and in early magical textbooks such as the *Vita Merlini* and *Prophecies of Merlin*.

RELATIONSHIP BETWEEN TAROT AND GOD FORMS

The Tarot Trumps also incorporate a number of classical and pagan god-forms or goddess-forms, and these are clarified by the polarity meditations suggested in our exercise above. There are certain specific images which always demand careful examination and explanation; these are DEATH, THE DEVIL, THE HANGED MAN. They may be understood by considering their polar relationship with their harmonic opposites, and by their derivation from early god forms.

In the *Vita Merlini* Merlin plays both The Fool, who asks naive questions and takes foolish steps around the Wheel of Life, and the

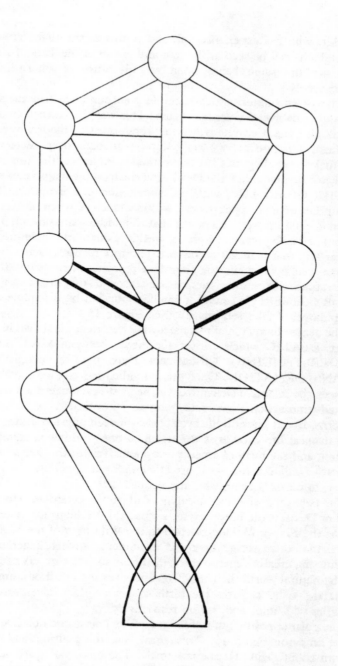

Figure 16.   The Tower and Strength, breaking and building.

Hermit, who has experienced all and retires to spiritual solitude. These Paths can be seen at the foot and crown of the Tree of Life; they are the same being upon an adventure of internalising consciousness.

His first encounter, which is the first encounter in true magical initiation, involves a Guardian figure. This was the Horned God of the pagan Celts (Cernunnos, who is worshipped by modern revival witches), a nature power, yet one who guarded deep secrets of spiritual power. Due to Christian orthodox influence, this image in the Tarot became titled 'the Devil', but the working magician sees it as THE GUARDIAN, with no connotation of corruption. The corruption or evil appears only within ourselves when we try to hoard or retain secrets and power that should be shared by all. This type of evil is so prevalent with the wealth of our world, culminating in warfare, that it needs no further description. But it arises from human weakness, while the Guardian protects inner secrets from desecration, yet admits the initiate through the interaction of GLORY-SEVERITY (mind or intellect purified by discipline and the removal of false self-image). (See Figure 15.)

The deeper harmonic of this harrowing experience is shown in the image DEATH, which crosses the Abyss between SEVERITY-UNDERSTANDING. This is not mere physical death, but TRANSFORMATION. Once the individual has crossed the abyss between the solar and stellar Worlds, he or she no longer lives in the limited transactional areas of regular outer-fixated or habitual patterns. In our physical life cycle, this is indeed physical death; but in a magical life cycle it is the death of one worldview, transformation, and the birth of a new perception. It is for this reason that the card *Death* is sometimes correctly employed in popular fortune-telling to mean 'a change for the better'.

The polar opposite, but fulfilling, Path to the Guardian (Horned God or Devil) is the Empress (see Figure 15). In the pagan systems, this is the Flower Maiden married to the Wild Man of the Woods. She is the potent yet gentle power of outgoing, giving, generating, modulating creative energy through the emotions (Mercy/Victory). In the natural world the Guardian supervises the death of animals, while the Lady controls the birth of plants: they have seasonal qualities of Winter and Spring respectively.

The polar opposite, but fulfilling, Path to Transformation (Death) is the Emperor (Figure 15). This reveals something curious and little known about DEATH: she is Female. The medieval figure of the skeleton and scythe, connected to Saturn/Chronos, replaces a pagan goddess of death and taking. She is the female power of breaking down, carrying the consciousness across the Abyss to the Great Mother (Understanding). Her partner is the outgoing creative god-form (Emperor) who crosses the Abyss in the opposite direction, bringing the stellar explosive energies across the deep to become life forms; these are mediated in turn by a goddess-form (Empress) as they proceed towards manifestation.

THE HANGED MAN

Three Trumps cross the universal abyss; Star, Temperance and the Hanged Man. The Abyss is the physical abyss of space between the individual stars and stellar systems, and in this sense these three Trumps link the solar-world and the stellar-world. But, in terms of life and consciousness, they cross the divide between supernal awareness (Crown, Wisdom, Understanding) and consciousness/energy expressed as physical entities through the forms of stars, solar systems, planets and their biospheres.

The Hanged Man shows the relationship between the Great Mother (Understanding) and the centrality of the Son of Light (Harmony or Beauty). The Mother is the infinite vessel of eternity, the Son is the spiritual centre of all Being mediating between supernal and infernal consciousness; hence his role as Saviour. The Tarot image shows a figure that hangs upside down, not through any contrived notion of abnegation, but because the awareness of this Path literally turns perception upside down and inside out. Time is no longer solar time; it becomes an understanding of stellar life-spans and their interconnection in the web of time/space/energy. The intuitions that arise from meditation upon this Path are similar to the theories proposed by modern physics, but this image and conceptual interaction have been employed in the Mysteries for many centuries.

In the *Vita Merlini* we find the Hanged Man as an emblem of the ritual Threefold Death, which was epitomised by the Crucifixion. He falls, hangs and drowns simultaneously; thus he falls across the Abyss, hangs as a bridge of inverted transformed consciousness from the branches of the Tree of Life, and submerges his head in the sea of energies that sustains the sun in the womb of eternity. It is most significant to note that the head, sacred to the Celts, is the seat of regular awareness, but that various means of disposing of the head (turning the awareness inwards) involve reversal of polarity.

The key words for this Trump are Understanding/Beauty, or Timeless Harmony, the Great Mother and the Son of Light. His apparent death is a sacrifice only to the uninitiated; he crosses the

163

centre of the Circle in magical art, so suspends all laws of time, space and energy.

TEMPERANCE

The fulfilling opposite to the Hanged Man is Temperance, in which a figure pours energy or essence from one vessel to another. While the image of the Hanged Man is catalytic, this image is analytic; it has a building or outward orientation, though it is still far beyond the cycle of manifest awareness. Key words are Wisdom/Beauty, the relationship and harmony of stellar cycles and outpouring energies. Whereas the Hanged Man relates those energies drawn inwards to the Great Mother, Temperance relates to energies expanding outwards from stellar realms to individual solar-worlds. Here the Father, or seeding power of Being, outpours energy into the vessel of the Son or solar consciousness. Both of these Trumps relate to the figure of the Saviour in all magic, religion or spiritual contemplation. The Hanged Man is withdrawn across the Abyss, while Temperance is the affirmation of outpouring power mediated through a solar balancing location.

Between the left and right hand paths of Hanged Man and Temperance, we find the Star, the direct connection between the Son of Light and the originating Spirit or Crown. It is significant that the Trump *Judgement*, sometimes seen as the last Judgement or universal resurrection, is placed across this stellar world, linking its ultimate polarities, crossing the Star at ninety degrees in our flat conceptual model. This interrelationship shows that death and resurrection exist on a cosmic scale, with the breathing in and out of the universe and worlds of Being. The mediating influence of the Saviour or Son of Light (a stellar being who also acts as the centrality for a solar/planetary system) links the trans-universal modes of Being (Supernal Spheres) with the transpersonal human consciousness (Infernal Spheres).

In modern magical arts we find the potential resurrection as a reality that enlivens the mind, soul and body, leading eventually to the paradoxical translation into other worlds. The literal orthodox resurrection is a medieval confusion derived from propaganda mingled with pagan philosophies which were still extant in the west either as literary remnants or as folklore; this type of resurrection is fiction, while the magical translation and its lesser harmonic of the transpersonal resurrection, are actual events within the reach of all who practise magical arts or inner disciplines.

164

METHODS OF USING TAROT IMAGES

The descriptions of polarity and the personal work pattern described above will take much effort and time to realise inwardly. In one sense they represent the life-work of each and every magician, hence the constant emphasis upon the open-ended nature of the symbolism; no one can live life for another, and this is particularly true in magical or spiritual disciplines, where teachers may only point the way. There are no guide books to inner experience, only signposts. The Tarot comprise a very effective set of images that act as signposts.

Visualisation of Tarot trumps is an enduring magical practice of unknown origin. As many of the images appear in the magical handbook of the *Vita Merlini* we may assume that they were in use prior to the twelfth century in Europe. Oral tradition suggests that they are very ancient indeed, and derive from intuition and seership.

Two basic methods are applied to Tarot images, plus a number of more advanced practices.

1) *Study and form,* a meditation upon the symbols assembled in the image. This method begins by assessing the contents of each image, usually with some preliminary tuition or guidance either from a book or from a teacher. In our next chapter a traditional method for learning from innerworld teachers is described, and this type of tuition is central to western magical art. Most of the western 'masters' exist in other dimensions accessible to the imagination, rather than as human teachers. Once the basic meaning and elements of an image are learnt, the magician meditates upon the image as shown on a card or picture. This type of meditation is conducted with eyes open, allowing the information acquired and the visual content of the image to fuse together through concentration upon the image and nothing else. Fresh intimations and ideas are generated by this method, which should be written out after the meditation session. As suggested above, once the student is familiar with the images, they may be worked in pairs, triads or cycles of relationship.

2) *'Path working'.* This method is loosely derived from Hebrew mystical and magical traditions, but is really part of the mainstream of inner visualisation that occurs in wisdom traditions worldwide. The striking visual images described in early texts preserved in medieval manuscripts or Celtic oral tradition are as valid for 'path-working' as Tarot images, but lack the systematic coherence until assembled upon the Tree of Life.

The magician meditates upon a Tarot image, assembling the symbols, qualities and correlations to the Tree of Life. He or she then passes onto a deeper mode of imaginative consciousness, in which the image comes to life in the inner vision, and is entered fully. In this type of work, although the session may begin with open eyes, the higher levels are undertaken with eyes closed.

Entering into the landscape or ambience of the Trump, the magician builds it as strongly as possible in the imagination; all the senses are deployed; sight in colour, sound, touch, taste, scent. This type of work can result in very dramatic inner experiences, and it is usual to set a time limit (not given by an outer clock but merely in the mind) and to provide a key phrase or movement (such as the Crossing described in our previous chapter) for exit. Two stages exist within this visionary technique:

a) *Constancy of image.* The image is held firmly in its original form as indicated by the card. Any changes or intrusions are firmly resisted by returning the imagination to the original image as practised in our meditation (1) above.

b) *Change of image.* After some preliminary work, certain changes may occur to the Tarot image; these will always be in keeping with the original meaning, and will not be disruptive or frivolous. If they do become so, the magician withdraws and recommences the exercise.

Any changes, or appearances of people or actions from people already within the image, should be remembered and noted. Such changes are often accompanied by intuitions upon the deeper meaning of the image.

In the method described (2a/b) it is unlikely and impractical to work with joint images or multiple images simultaneously. We may, however, assemble Trumps or Paths that have polar or cyclical relationships and pass from one to the other in the inner vision. This method requires practice at dissolving an inner vision and gently replacing it with the next phase. The cards make useful guiding symbols for this, as it is sometimes necessary (in early training) to open the eyes and review the next Trump to be visualised.

Journeys of this sort sometimes develop into rather passive trips around the inner world, and they should never be conducted in such a manner. Traditionally the Fool travels around the Tree of Life, from Earth to Heaven and back to Earth. This journey is partly carried out by the assembly of symbols given in our earlier exercise where the magician learns the attributes of each Trump and its place upon the Tree of Life. During further work, selected relationships of Trumps are employed, while at an even later period of development, these may be again assembled into a whole Tree, often with a quite different inner effect.

INVOCATION

The Trumps or Paths may also be used for magical invocation, and a basic method could be applied as follows:

1) Open the Circle.
2) Open a Gate (between physical Pillars if necessary) which becomes the Path, with each of its Spheres located upon a Pillar.
3) Within this Gate, visualise the Trump, after briefly invoking the powers of each Sphere at either extreme side of the Gate.
4) Always treat the image and energies present as real, never assume that they are 'merely symbolic'. Thus in very formal ritual bows or signs of blessing (such as the Cross or Hexagram) are often employed during invocations.
5) Meditate upon the presence, particularly its relationship to divinity and the creative will of Being.
6a) Dissolve the energies by circling and dissipating the power to the outer world prior to closing the Circle. Alternatively:
6b) Make a blessing sign over the image and power invoked (using a formula such as the *Invocation of the Son of Light* or more traditionally in orthodox magic the Lord's Prayer). The being invoked is formally invited to withdraw, while visualising it passing through the Gates and back into the Void.
7) The gates are closed formally, and the Circle dissolved.

DISTANCE CONTACT

While trivial fortune-telling is not encouraged in the western traditions, there are a number of methods by which Trumps are used to attune the consciousness to distant events, places or people. Once the initiate has worked with the images, there are various experiments that may be carried out along these lines, with the firm rule that no imposition should be made upon another individual such as forcing the energies of a Trump or other set of symbols upon them in your imagination.

One of the most basic methods is simply to lay out ten cards in the shape of the Tree of Life. Meditate briefly upon each one in order, bearing in mind the nature of the subject which you wish to assess, learn about, or contact. If this type of work results in confusion it should be abandoned until further inner understanding and connection to the Trumps has been built up.

It cannot be emphasised too strongly that this type of exercise is of far less value than the essential training work of magic, and that it should not consume time and energy better spent in meditation or study. Despite its superficial aim, inner realisations often arise during such associative exercises, so they are not entirely trivial in purpose.

CONVERSATIONS AND STORY-TELLING

One of the most hallowed and ancient ways of using images, and undoubtedly one of the purposes to which early Tarot cards were put, is in simple conversation or story-telling.

Conversation

An image (such as a Trump) is selected and briefly meditated upon. The magician then strikes up an imaginary conversation with whoever or whatever is in the image. This is a natural imaginative game (children are familiar with it) and not anything to do with 'spiritualism'. Such Conversations can give rise to valuable insights, information and experience; on a deeper level they may act as an interface for levels of consciousness which may not yet be accessible to the magician.

Story-telling

A set of images, between four and ten in number, are taken from the pack and laid out either in a pattern (such as the Circle or the Tree of Life) or, less effectively, in order of appearance. The magician then proceeds to make a story out of the sequence shown. This tale will contain magical insights, and a wealth of symbolic material. Such games are far from superficial, and make a more productive and healthy use of the visual imagination than merely watching television. The antiquity of this method is such that it long predates modern techniques of association developed in materialist psychology. Furthermore it is not aimed exclusively at personal insight or therapy; the stories generated are drawn from cosmic transpersonal symbols, therefore they have many deep levels of meaning. As with the method of Conversation described above, Story-telling can lead to significant innerworld contact. This leads us to our next chapter, in which innerworld contact is dealt with in detail.

18 INNERWORLD CONTACTS

An enduring concept in magical arts through the centuries, worldwide, is that of the spirit or innerworld contact. This may be in the form of an exchange, tuition, advice, communication, or even as part of an assembly of physical and metaphysical persons as in religious ceremonies. There are many traditions that include such contacts, often with widely differing opinions and methods, yet all agree on one fundamental premise; innerworld beings exist. They are entities which are uniquely or collectively conscious in dimensions which are accessible through the imagination; through higher modes of awareness. Magical arts are employed to communicate and work with such beings, sometimes to a very refined pattern or with long-term effects lasting through centuries.

It is not possible to go far into the practice of magic without encountering such beings. We should examine the theory and practice of innerworld contact, and put it into our modern context of magical arts. It is not as strange, sinister, ignorant or naïve as is often assumed.

INNERWORLDS DEFINED

Before proceeding, we must establish a general definition of the term 'innerworlds'. Although the word 'innerworld' is modern, born out of the dubious relationship between magical arts and materialist psychology, the concept is ancient; it is inherent within the human psyche. *An Innerworld is a firmly defined and identifiable state or place or world which may be perceived by the inward direction of attention.*

The fundamental arts of concentration, meditation and visualisation all lead consciousness to change its direction, moving *inwards* rather than fixating *outwards* at it does in daily habitual life.

In general meditation, as in modern mental therapy, the preliminary areas explored are those to the individual psyche (thoughts, emotions, responses). Innerworlds, however, are perceived through the imaginative visualising faculties, and are *not* part of the individual psyche.

Innerworlds may also be contacted through ritual work, whereby a pattern is set up that opens a Gate (a resonance of energy that attunes the imagination and a number of other inner faculties to a specific mode of consciousness). The opening of Gates is central to magical work, bringing the outer world into contact with the inner worlds through physical location. The building of sacred sites, temples and churches is a physical expression of such practices. In certain structures, such as the medieval Abbeys, the fusion of physics and metaphysics reaches remarkable heights of achievement.

Innerworlds are consistent; they are as unique and enduring as outer 'worlds', lands, structures or organisations. Many of them endure through extremely long periods of time; others are all but inaccessible to the questing human perception. Some innerworlds are well known through collective tradition: Faeryland or Elfland; magical islands; certain Temples or gathering places. They are upheld both by folklore and by historical magical practices. Other worlds or inner places are highly specialised and known only to the magical orders who work with them.

We must be careful not to confuse inner imaginal worlds with the products of the fantasy or entertainment industry. A 'world' in a fantasy film or novel may have certain resonances that connect it to magical innerworlds, but it is not such a world in its own right. Most 'worlds' in fantasy are ephemeral. It is only on rare occasions where a work of art has consciously or unconsciously attuned to a specific innerworld that such fantastical visions may be valid for magical practices.

A simple general rule is this: if you are reading a novel or watching a film, the fantasy world generated will merely be entertainment, even if it encapsulates many magical or ethical truths. If you are meditating or visualising and a coherent world is contacted, this is a true innerworld which can be experienced by many individual entities; magical tradition suggests that some of these worlds are more real than our own collective world.

In serious work with magical arts, the use of fantastical fiction for meditation or visualisation should be discouraged, as it dissipates the energies. While being good entertainment 'magical fiction' is not to be confused with magical practice. The unwary visualiser can waste endless time travelling on totally frivolous fantasy trips; these are

171

merely one remove from the more pernicious practice of distorting the perception through the use of psychedelic drugs.

Having gone some way towards defining inner worlds, we reach the inevitable point, so frequently encountered in magic, at which the individual must attempt to experience such matters rather than merely read about them. (A list of recordings for guided visualisation is given in the Bibliography.)

MAGIC, PSYCHOLOGY AND INNERWORLD CONTACTS

In materialist terms beings that live in imaginal dimensions are either expressions of a fragmented psyche, or pathological delusions. Some modern schools of mental therapy, such as Psychosynthesis, which draws a great deal of its methodology from magical and mystical traditions, admit to personalisation of images for psychic growth. Yet even these advanced forms of psychology will not admit any independent validity to the beings that modern magicians call 'innerworld contacts'.

The working magician must be careful not to confuse personified aspects of his or her own psyche (the greedy child, the wise old man, the sensual lover) with the possibility that specific entities may use human or other forms to stimulate our imagination and to communicate with us. There is no doubt that one of the lasting properties of human consciousness is the ability to take *energies* and represent them as *entities* within the imagination; in magical tradition there are also entities which stimulate energies within the psyche... but remain independent of it. Such entities, beings, exist in the innerworld dimensions of consciousness/energy that are usually inaccessible to waking human awareness.

To make this matter more confusing in the initial stages of analysis, the innerworld contacts are of a number of different types. Some are vitally important in the magial process of growth through interaction, while others are merely trivial and distracting. This picture is clarified and rendered less disturbing by a simple comparison to daily life; we meet many people and creatures regularly, but not all of them are important in our lives, even though each and every one is ultimately part of our totality of experience.

The traditional systems of magic may be summarised by the table that follows, giving basic areas or types of being that may be part of magical communication. In general practice it is not necessary to learn detailed tables of correspondence for each class of being,

172

although this often seems to be the case when we examine early magical texts in which such tables feature prominently. In daily use of the fundamental disciplines, a working magician builds a style or pattern of creativity, just as an artist or musician will, in time, develop a style of work or performance. This growth comes only with experience, and although detailed lists and technical matters need to be attacked vigorously and incorporated into the psyche, they are eventually refined and relegated to an unconscious area of use. In the development of outer skills this also applies, for hands soon act smoothly in motions which (at the outset) seemed highly difficult to the beginner. A similar process of learning and distillation applies in the magical arts.

If we condense the traditional lists, we arrive at the following:

'OTHER' WORLDS	ORDERS OF NON-HUMAN BEINGS
MANIFEST WORLD	ORDERS OF HUMAN BEINGS and OTHER CREATURES
INNER AND ANCESTRAL WORLDS	ORDERS OF EX-HUMAN BEINGS
INNER SPIRITUAL WORLDS	ORDERS OF TRANSHUMAN BEINGS
WORLD OF NATURE	ORDERS OF ELEMENTALS and NATURE SPIRITS
WORLD OF SOLAR SYSTEM	ORDERS OF ANGELS or SOLAR/PLANETARY BEINGS
WORLD OF UNIVERSE	ORDERS OF ARCHANGELS or STELLAR BEINGS

Each category may be summarised briefly as follows (see also Figure 17).

'Other' Worlds

Dimensions in which beings are encountered who are not, and never have been, human. These include human forms such as god and goddess images, animal forms or combined forms, or specific magical beings such as Guardians, Guides or Faery beings. Additional to such entities which have a collective expression in

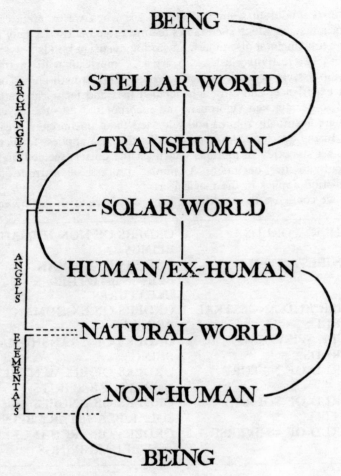

Figure 17. Cosmic and Universal psyche.

traditional legends and magical tuition, there are also many other types of being which may (more rarely) be encountered by the consciousness of the magician or group. Such beings exist in worlds or dimensions which are not usually related to the human life-patterns, though magical experiments have been conducted in relationship with such beings. As a general rule, utterly non-human-related entities are a waste of the magicians' valuable energies and time; they simply do not respond to our efforts in a reliable or comprehensible manner.

Manifest World

Our collective world, this is frequently and foolishly despised by the beginner in magic or mystical arts who seeks to escape. The manifest world is an extremely powerful magical world, which may have potent effects upon the inner worlds. More obviously, it is the world in which we spend a great deal of our consciousness and energies, and we should seek to make our contacts in this world as effective and harmonious as possible. Traditionally the world of matter, the collective sphere of consciousness-on-planet is assembled from the gates or contact areas of innumerable other or inner worlds. Any contact in the manifest world may have profound magical effect if it is properly utilised and understood.

One of the major aims of magical arts is to rebalance and beautify the world, beginning within the individual magician. In this specific sense, we may make inner contact with other humans who harmonise with our own intentions; many apparently remarkable meetings and coincidences occur in magical arts due to this simple property of harmonic resonance between certain people. We should not, therefore, exclude humans from our innerworld contact list. Conversely, there is a long-standing and well-justified ban on attempting to force inner contact with unknowing persons; this is as much an assault as any physical assault.

Inner and Ancestral Worlds

These are the areas of collective consciousness which perpetuate certain key motifs, symbols, persons in image, and other beings relating to the long-term relationship between humans and the land. One very potent and specific method of magic known in western culture employs these contacts: the UnderWorld Initiation. There is significant difference between this type of innerworld and use of similar areas as related by psychology; the first is an enduring set of dimensions which are inhabited by beings with will; the second is that fragment of these worlds that is encapsulated within our individual unconscious awareness. In the Ancestral and Inner Worlds we meet ex-human beings, advanced entities who once lived in the collective physical world, but who have become transformed through experience or magical or spiritual arts. This transformation enables them to live within dimensions that are held together by very specific symbols that relate environment, people, and often employ certain unique physical locations. This type of being is found repeatedly in legend, folklore and mythology. In the west our classic

175

examples are people who have a historical origin, but have also become endowed with magical and mythical ambience. Examples might be Thomas Rhymer, certain 'Arthurian' heroes, Fair Rosamund, Merlin, Doctor Dee, Thomas More, Robert Kirk. People of this sort, and there will be many that history does not record, have advanced beyond the human state of physical incarnation, but remain close to our world as teachers. Our own ancestors are included in this area where history and poetry merge...paradoxically we are all ex-humans if we consider our previous lives.

The dangers of such ancestral or national contacts lie in excess of racial fervour, a type of imbalance common among weak-willed and elitist occultists. The strengths in such contacts are drawn from the intimate relationship to the land and to the very best distillation of collective wisdom and magical experience.

It is at this stage that we must remember that such contacts are not mere 'spiritualism'. They are very refined and active types of magical work in which beings interact with one another, often involving more than one world. The silly notion of advice from some vague spirit world plays no part in magical arts; furthermore there are certain technical flaws in the practice of spiritualism which all competent magicians are wary of, particularly the debilitating effect that so-called 'spirit guides' have upon their human mediums. In magical art such parasitic contacts are not encouraged, and if they do arise are regarded as highly undesirable, and are broken up.

Discretion is achieved through the tuning and symbolism of the magical circle, and the quality of meditation and mediation employed. There is no vague or passive reception in magical work, and certainly no concept whatsoever of subservience to metaphysical or imaginative beings.

Inner Spiritual Worlds

These are where we encounter highly-evolved beings who transcend the matrices of land or even of planet. In religions these are known as saints or on a more exalted level as divinities who were once human. Such beings are transhuman; they have transcended their humanity and become citizens of a greater consciousness. In some magical circles these are called inner plane adepts, in others they are termed Sacred Kings, while in others they are Masters. This level of entity is not, of course, exclusively male, and it is unfortunate that much of our vocabulary is still tainted by a male-dominant culture and religion. Similar terms are applied to beings in our previous category

(Inner and Ancestral Worlds) though this is sometimes erroneous.

Transhuman beings are metaphysical entities of advanced aware-ness, free consciousness reaching its limits of individual identity, close to the source of Being itself. They are androgynous, though they may appear to the inner vision as either male or female. Such encounters are rare, and magicians should not fool themselves into thinking that every impulse from inner contact is derived from such beings.

In traditional magic, a chain or hierarchy of communication was said to exist, in which the more advanced entities worked through intermediaries who in turn reached to human or sub-human levels. This is an interesting teaching, for it reflects a pattern inherent in the individual psyche, whereby levels or states of awareness inter-penetrate one another. In magic, the human microcosm is a reflection of the macrocosm of divine existence; in simple terms this means that highly powerful spiritual beings will come into contact with use either through lesser entities, or through appearing in the guise or form of such entities. It is often found in advanced magical work that inner contacts fuse together, and a new being appears in the consciousness of the magician or group.

This type of magic is remarkably effective if it is a spontaneous and natural event, but tedious and preposterous if aimed and contrived by human conceit. We can see illnesses resulting from such imbalance in the various cults that proclaim sole ownership of God...and this type of weakness is also found in individual magical adepts who believe that they and they alone hold the keys to divinity.

Transhuman beings appear in magical work for very specific group operations at times of great crisis, or at key moments in the turning of solar or stellar synchronicity. Much of the original art of astrology was concerned with connections between the outer world, the inner worlds, and stellar patterns. Our modern astrology has lost this metaphysical foundation, while retaining many of the remark-ably accurate derivations that are really secondary to the main purpose of the art.

INNERWORLDS AND INDIVIDUAL STATES OF CONSCIOUSNESS

The summary of worlds and beings in magical art divides into two specific areas: non-human through to transhuman, and elemental through to stellar. There is an interplay between these areas that defies any hard-and-fast boundaries of definition; as this interplay is central to the philosophy and practice of magic, we must examine it further before summarising the worlds or dimensions from Elemental to Stellar consciousness.

Figure 18 shows how the awareness of worlds and beings, non-human to transhuman, relates to a magical psychological map of consciousness. The circles of the diagram merge into one another without hard boundaries, and correspond to meditative and ritually-defined states of consciousness while *simultaneously* referring to magical worlds and independent beings. There is no suggestion that the worlds are merely products of the individual psyche, or that the psyche is limited by the definition of the worlds. The apparently limited individual human being is a reflection of the unlimited conscious universe; the worlds, beings and the psyche therefore are

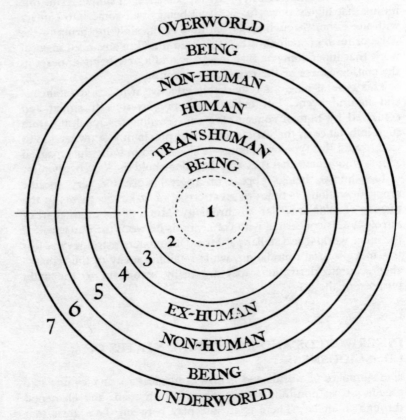

Figure 18. *Worlds and Beings.*

inseparably merged. The apparent limitations come from the habitual barriers and filters in regular awareness... barriers which are of themselves magical and therefore imaginary.

We could summarise the diagram as follows:

1) The centre of our being is Non-Being.

2) Non-Being polarises into Being. This is a formless and timeless state of consciousness in which humans may ultimately find their true spiritual essence.

3) Formless timeless Being reflects itself through interaction with Non-Being. This gives rise to holographic or holistic entities which are harmonically derived from the original consciousness. In the human meditative modes of awareness such entities are found to be transhuman; they are only apprehended in a higher mode of awareness which may be gained by various methods and disciplines, one of which is ritual magic.

4) Spiritual entities (transhuman beings) interact and reflect expressions of themselves which we understand as human and ex-human beings. Such reflections are apprehended in meditation, through imagination, in physical contact.

5) Beyond the human rate or state of manifestation/reflection, consciousness re-approaches its original root in Being out of Non-Being. In this set of worlds, corresponding to magical and meditational psychic modes of the UnderWorld, various orders of non-human beings are encountered. Also present in this region of the psyche/universal reflective matrix are non-human entities of stellar elemental nature. They are encountered in various aspects through each and every mode of consciousness or world, for they partake of the Archetype or matrix by which Non-Being becomes Being.

6) By directing awareness inwards or downwards the human entity emerges out of the UnderWorld dimensions into the realm of pure Being. Paradoxically this is also expressed as the manifest outer world; the individual who has been transformed through magical experiences of this category apprehends Divinity in Matter, or in traditional Kabbalistic terminology, the Crown unified with the Kingdom.

7) Beyond this state the consciousness dissolves into Non-Being.

It must be emphasised that maps such as the one shown are not intended as definitive or authoritative hierarchical sets of rules; they are merely guiding outlines derived from repeated inner experience, taught in magical and mystical traditions. Many literally-minded students or critics of magical arts fail to understand that such maps need not be integrated with one another or that they may even contradict one another. The integration and realisation happens within the consciousness, not upon a piece of paper.

HOW INNERWORLDS ARE PERPETUATED

Innerworlds are created and maintained through collective skilled manipulation of Imaginative power. Such worlds, reflected and sculpted through the areas defined by our cycle of manifestation described above (the seven circles or interpenetrating states of consciousness) are made from *images*. The images are employed by the will of groups of entities; when energised in this manner, such imaginative structures define the end-product of archetypical matrices. These archetypical matrices are the seed-patterns of the Universal Imagination...the interaction between Non-Being and Being.

Traditionally the Fourfold Pattern or Circle/Sphere is the archetype of patterns, the foundation and origin of reflection through the worlds; it defines the phases of ultimate consciousness or Divinity, and expresses a cycle of Four Elements or consciousness-in-matter.

Through the willed application of images, a construct such as a temple may be an expression or statement of the relative pattern of the solar system. This in turn is an expression of the archetype of cyclical manifestation and de-manifestation. Mystical and magical visions move towards a merging of creation and destruction, hence the apocalyptic tone of many mystical texts. Using our example of a temple, we know that physical buildings (be they classical temples, stone circles, earthworks or cathedrals) are intentionally planned to show forth mathematical, stellar or seasonal patterns with magical and metaphysical implications.

An innerworld temple, however, is an imaginative construct that endures independently of outer time cycles in the material expressed world. It is upheld by collective imagination, modifying archetypes.

All worlds, inner and outer, partake of the Four Elements or Four Powers. These Four are the phases of the archetype or matrix by which universal consciousness reflects itself into increasingly complex patterns of imaginative expression.

We may now continue with our summary of the worlds, and move on to the second area, that of Elemental through to Stellar beings.

ELEMENTAL TO STELLAR BEINGS
See Figure 17.

The World of Nature

This is where the much publicised (and little understood) Element-als and Nature spirits may be contacted. It is, as must be obvious, an aspect of our Manifest world...yet it is an innerworld or series of innerworlds simultaneously. In early training, the subjective re-sponse to the world of nature is extremely important as many of the beings in this sequence of dimensions can energise and purify the human imagination. The interplay of bio-electrical energies that is so important in magical work is often realigned by our healthy contact with natural forces; though there is no need to attribute each and every natural stimulus to an innerworld being. This last problem of over-attribution is common in early stages of magical work when enthusiasm over new discoveries tends to cloud the action of common sense.

Elementals are entities of limited uni-directional conscious-energy. As the name implies, they are primarily attuned to one of the Four Elements of Air, Fire, Water or Earth, and traditionally they play an important role in magical invocation. Modern occultism seems to be slightly confused over the role of Elementals...they are sometimes regarded as beneficial, and sometimes as uncontrollable pests. The confusion arises because the theory has increasingly been taken out of its proper context.

Elementals are part of the harmonious worldview developed in ancient cultures in which Nature, Solar system and Stars harmonise with one another. The Elemental, therefore, is an entity that is only defined by *relationship;* it is a holographic unit of the greater entity of conscious-energy from which it derives.

In terms of innerworld contact Elementals may convey inform-ation or reaction to the magician, or they may be automatic aspects of a ritual or meditation upon the Elements. There is an increasing tendency in modern magical arts to replace the working concept of Elements as entities with the concept of the Elements within human-kind. Due to the harmonic qualities which run through the worlds of Elementals, Nature, Planetary and Solar beings and Stellar beings, we may lose the ancient holistic vision of unified worlds if we assume that the Elements are only inner qualities.

In traditional magic, a Circle is drawn, and its Four Quarters are energised by a series of innerworld beings. The first beings in this holism are often Elementals, basic entities of conscious energy that attune to the Four Elements.

Elementals are limited in their flow of consciousness, but potentially unlimited in the release of energy. Our relationship with such entities, and with their reflections and energies within ourselves, must be one of balance and poise, rather than of 'control'. Control of Elementals is often discussed in popular occultism, but is as spurious as our materialist concept of controlling Nature; indeed, it is the same fallacy removed to metaphysical or psychic dimensions. Balanced interaction is possible, but control through conflict only results in an increasing factor of imbalance. One of the great weaknesses of literary occultism in the west is its emphasis upon 'authority' and 'power'; during the latter part of the twentieth century we are paying a terrible price for this concept, materialised as famine, pollution, and the threat of appalling destruction from a perversion of nuclear energy into weapons of war – nuclear energy is literally star energy.

Nature Spirits are extremely popular in the fringe areas of magical work, mainly due to the vague and rather ridiculous notions written about fairies and spirits during the early years of 'spiritualism' in the nineteenth century. If we compare the nature spirit and fairies of modern popular conception with those of tradition (such as the description found in Robert Kirk's *Secret Commonwealth*) we find two very different pictures; one vapid, cosy and weak, the other wilful, disturbing and strong.

In magical work, nature spirits are entities of limited but specific consciousness relating to certain localities and life forms. They are not Elementals in the sense described above, as they comprise combinations of elements. A local goddess or water-spirit, such as was worshipped in pagan times, is actually a combination of the elements within a localised form; yet at the same time she is a holistic resonance of the Great Goddess, the feminine principle of Being. A tree-spirit or dryad is a limited but individually-conscious entity accumulated from the energy of certain trees. The variety of Nature spirits is boundless as the variety of Nature.

Magicians do not usually seek to employ nature spirits in group ritual, unless the working is orientated specifically towards an end directly in keeping with the consciousness of nature spirits. In other words, while we may perceive such entities with our inner vision, and interact with them in meditation upon the wonders of the natural world, we would not employ them in consciousness-changing rituals...the type of working which forms at least two-thirds of magical ritual operation. The reasoning behind this is simple and direct; nature spirits are on a level of awareness which is lower than our own, and certain typical imbalances found in magicians (particularly pagan and nature practitioners) often arise from wedding part of the psyche to the consciousness of a nature spirit.

In the sophisticated pagan religions magical acts of this type were indeed undertaken regularly; but they were supported by a deeper philosophy and theurgy than that which is known in modern paganism.

The most profound aspect of the world of Nature is that it can help us to apprehend Being through the simple and unaffected patterns of natural life. When human culture has proven impossible to tolerate or forgive, for the moment, we may still find glory in the land and its non-human inhabitants, ranging from simple plants to complex entities based upon magical locations. But we should never seek to escape into Nature and deny our human heritage; this is shown very clearly in the magical allegory of Merlin who was driven insane by human warfare. He fled to the wildwood, but eventually discovered that true peace comes from a merging of the wild with the cultured...in Merlin's story this is demonstrated through a cycle of adventures culminating in the building of a stellar observatory in the woods, to which Merlin and his company retire to undertake spiritual contemplation. They reject both the raw wildwood and the unhealthy city, but seek truth in a harmonious construct which brings stars and nature into union through human mediation. This allegory is the perfect model of a balanced magical system of growth and entry into spiritual maturity.

World of the Solar System

We now begin to move spatially outwards from the planet, though this may also be experienced by moving inwards and downwards in meditation and visualisation. Our next harmonic level of dimensions or collective world is that of the solar system; the Sun and attendant planets, other bodies, and various life forms. This world encapsulates the world of nature but also interpenetrates it.

Traditionally we find orders of angels and solar or planetary beings in this world. Although the term 'angel' seems to imply religious orthodoxy, we are using it here in a technical sense; just as elementals are entities expressing a fourfold-cycle in the natural world, so do angels express it in the solar and planetary world. The

183

term is so loosely applied in general usage that an 'angel' has come to mean almost anything supernatural but benevolent. . .excluding of course angels of death and fallen angels! In magical work, the definitions are usually more precise, and derived from enduring traditions of spiritual education; an angel is actually a *messenger* carrying the will of the Creator. We might say that while Elementals are the thought-entities of nature, angels are the thought-entities of the solar system.

If we take the consciousness of the solar system as a unified being, with the star (our sun) at its heart, angels are the *enabling* or *carrying* forms for both its energies and its imagination. Hence in western religion they are called the messengers of God, while in esoteric symbolism they are the communicating and modifying channels of conscious-energy encountered by humans when they apprehend a solar mode of awareness, or enter the solar world in their imaginations.

Contrary to popular fantasy, angels do not appear to men and declare the will of God, at least not in the literal pedantic sense. The contact with an angelic being stimulates the imagination to a series of reflections which represent the message or mode of consciousness inherent in the angel itself. If such contacts appear as blazing lights and trumpets, it is usually because we are not ready for them, and are unable to mediate or translate their message. In magical art, the building of a circle and the repeated work with images, innerworld contacts and elemental energies, train the magician to attune sensibly to higher contacts, be they transhuman spiritual beings or angels and archangels.

Angels, therefore, relate the cycles, phases and patterns of the solar consciousness, carrying such energies through the entire *world* which comprises the Sun and all planets, bodies, life forms and inner worlds attuned to it or deriving from it.

In the majority of magical and mystical initiations, it is the solar consciousness that is found as the highest or most intense realisation; it is at this level that we cross over into the next innerworld or harmonic level, for the Sun is also a Star.

World of the Universe

In this harmonic level of being, we encounter archangels or stellar entities. Our Sun, the centrality of the solar system, is one of innumerable stars. In metaphysics, each star is a being of consciousness; the physical energetic form that radiates into space is merely one presentation of a star...in magical art many other forms are experienced through inner vision.

Our intuition regarding world-relationships suggests a harmonic sequence that equates to a spatial, ultimately spherical, map. Elements, Angels, Archangels; or Planet, Sun system, Stars. Human beings are often placed somewhere between the angels and the elements, yet the human consciousness is said to pervade all worlds, for it is a unique reflection of the creative Being. Figure 19 shows this relationship, and the merging of non-human through to transhuman consciousness with the spheres of the elementals, angels and archangels.

The enclosing ring or sphere, that of stellar consciousness,

Figure 19.   Three harmonic inclusive Spheres or Rings of Consciousness.
3) ARCHANGELIC or Stellar-Solar Sphere (encompasses all).
2) ANGELIC or Solar-Lunar Sphere (encompasses Sphere 1).
1) ELEMENTAL or Lunar-Material Sphere (encompasses seed of Being).

185

traditionally represented by archangels, includes all three areas of harmonic definition; the innermost is the material world (our planet in our Earth-based reference system) which, paradoxically, is furthest away from yet closest to the source of Being at the centre and circumference. In magical work, particularly the basic rituals which are never superseded, the Four Archangels, each representing a quarter of the circle or sphere of Being, are invoked. The reasoning behind this is simple but not foolish; the Four primal communicating or enabling modes of conscious energy run through all existence.

Before taking the matter any further, we must realise that the use of 'Archangels' in modern magical practices is not merely a relic of Gnostic-Christian religion. The Four entities are inherent in any magical system, and prior to the historical influx of Judeo-Christian and oriental religious terminology, other symbols, names, terms, were employed to effect the same ends. Any good reference book on comparative religion or theosophy will offer endless relationships between differing terms for similar metaphysical states or spiritual beings worldwide; there is no need for the working magician to be intellectually aware of such word games, least of all to employ them in magical art.

When some experience has been gained in magical invocation, it is possible to use a variety of symbols for similar forces. The great Archangel Gabriel, for example, is situated in the West of the circle; he/she presides over all matters connected to Love, Cups or vessels, Fulfilment, maturity and the element of Water (see Figures 2 and 8). This figure of an Archangel may be replaced by invocation of a goddess who represents the same qualities. In revivals of Celtic symbolism, the figure of Briggidda has been employed as a focus for consciousness and energy in the West; in Buddhism the circle is divided into four aspects of Buddha, one for each mystical direction. The precision of the image or its cultural origins are of less importance than its coherent relationship to the physical and metaphysical powers that it represents. In the case of Archangels or any other cycle of images or concepts, they are cyclical parts of a whole; they are, poetically speaking, the dream-cycle of Creation. Archangels are one practical way of defining Four Primary Powers of Being; powers which are never static or rigid, but in a constant state of flux.

Just as Angels are the enablers or messengers of higher consciousness in a solar-system, so are Archangels the enablers of the same power through the stellar world; which is the entire universe.

What, then, is the difference between Archangels and god or

goddess forms, if they can replace one another in human symbolism? The difference is apparent in practice rather than in theory; a god or goddess form, or any similar magical image, tends to act in a composite manner built up not only of the power and consciousness that it represents, but of human usage and aspiration, through the ages, that is embedded in such an image. Just as innerworlds are built up and maintained by imagination moulding specific archetypes, so are magical images or god forms augmented by the imagination and by regular religious practice.

Archangels, angels and elementals are convenient words to employ for pure energetic entities that are not necessarily filtered through regional, cultural or environmental god-forms. We could, very likely, apply the concept of the Archangel if we were suddenly resident upon a planet in the distant galaxies; but the goddess Briggidda would be quite unlikely to put in an appearance, as she has strictly environmental qualities inherent in her entity.

The images of archangels found in orthodox religion tend to be localised and often confused; but they are vague echoes of four primal entities of universal consciousness. In highly-intellectual mystical systems, the numbers of angels and archangels are proliferated through mathematical calculation and the premise of various worlds that each have such beings inherent within them; for practical purposes the magician tends to sidestep such complexities. Magic comes from simple and powerful primal patterns; any detailed complexities are moving in the wrong direction, back towards an outwardly-fixated consciousness.

We can conclude our summary of the innerworlds and their being with one basic rule: the more direct and simple the magical ritual, the more likely it is to attune to the highest modes or worlds of conscious energy.

THE REALITY OF INNERWORLD CONTACTS

Many people simply cannot accept that such entities or levels of existence are 'real'; indeed, this debate over apparent reality is not confined to materialist sceptics, it has run through mystical speculation and magical or spiritual philosophy for as long as humankind has sought answers to questions about the nature of being. It must be stressed that in magical work the above orders or categories are not, and never have been, considered as mere formulations of the individual or group psyche. They are not personifications, but what might be loosely called metaphysical or non-material persons. This imaginative approach is the one and only secret of magic; the rest comes with practice.

But the magician also employs personifications, images and archetypes (in both the modern psychological and the true meaning of the word) knowing full well that these are shapes sculpted from the imagination. Such shapes or forms or images are the human interface for relationship to energies that we may not face unveiled; hence the superficially hierarchical systems of magical symbolism or devolution of energies from Divinity to Humanity. The linear quality, however, is an illusion borne of literary limitations; true magical education is oral and practical. The forms or filters within the imagination act as matrices for energy; as *beings* they have considerable independence and range of behaviour, but thought-forms (personifications and selected images or psychological archetypes) are not spiritual entities independent of the magician or ritual group creating them. They may attune very closely to such independent entities, and in many ritual workings, the image eventually is infilled or enabled by a true entity of a higher order. Put more simply, our image of an angel as a being in white robe with wings is rather absurd, but with certain refinements such as colour, expression, emotional content, even such a stereotyped image may be enlivened by a true angelic contact. It is worth noting that human-like images create a very powerful psychic reaction within us, even if intellectually, socially or scientifically they seem unsatisfactory.

To the beginner, this array of orders, images and interactions is baffling; yet with a certain amount of practice the magician builds selective filters in his or her psyche (just as we do in everyday life) whereby only those contacts of most relevance can appear to the inner vision or field of awareness. This is the meaning of the Triangle of Art, a medieval magical system, in which secrets, or beings, are manifested and contained. The triangle is the combination of imagination, concentration and intuition. The last quality, intuition, plays a great part in advanced magic, where contacts and inner energies are felt rather than visually symbolised. Intuition is the highest spiritual expression of the element of Earth . . . the power of touching.

There are a number of different ways to tune in to an innerworld contact; all such methods are embodied in the Five Fundamentals described in an earlier chapter. Appendix I is an exercise designed to put the magician in contact with specific teaching entities employed in western traditions of esoteric work. Initially this material may appear to be an exercise in therapeutic visualisation; but with balanced effort it comes alive and generates a real contact that leads to valuable communication and exchange.

While dealing with the issue of reality and the innerworld beings, we could consider briefly what we mean when we talk about a 'real' person in the daily round of life. If such a real person is someone who has a coherent, tangible and consistent pattern or identity which is found to be reliable, then we are all utterly unreal. Indeed, most of us are crude assemblies of stereotypical semi-persons (sometimes called sub-personalities in psychology) which hide clumsily behind a mask...the personality presented to others. Many real people in the outer world are far more ephemeral and far less alive than the inner-world beings encountered in magical perception and experience. Innerworld beings do not live under the fantasy-cloud that befogs regular psychic interaction for most of us; eventually the magician has his or her perceptions cleansed by interaction with the elements and the beings that resonate just beyond the range of regular routine awareness.

There is a simple rule in magical contact work; do not bother to debate the so-called reality of your contacts, but do behave as if they are real at the time of communication or interaction. Like people in the outer world, innerworld contacts will come and go; some will prove to be important, others will be fleeting encounters. Intellectual debate is meaningless in magical art, it can carry us only so far. But this does not imply that we should abandon scepticism, analysis or sound common sense. An innerworld contact that proposes absurd suggestions is just as dangerous as any imbalanced personality making absurd suggestions in the outer world. If a contact appears to be absurd, the magician challenges it; often the image and message will transform if correctly challenged or channelled. Modern occultism has more or less abandoned this element of magical ritual, which featured strongly in the curious grimoires of medieval ceremonial magic, or in folk tales.

Behind the transformation of innerworld beings is a deep mystical knowledge that power may express itself through either negative or positive forms; an angel may be a fallen angel or demon simultane-ously; a blessed ancestor may be a phantom; but if correctly chan-nelled by harmonious magical patterns, they inevitably transform into the mode set by the symbolism or consciousness of the magician. Any spurious entities flee away or dissolve, for they are only shadows. The rather ridiculous notion of names of power that compel subservience from supernatural beings is really a corruption of this wisdom teaching.

19 CONCLUSION: THE FUTURE OF MAGICAL ARTS

There are no 'conclusions' to be drawn at the close of a book of this sort. It is possible, however, to consider the future of magical arts in western culture.

At the most material phase of our civilisation, we have a considerable revival of interest in magic, though generally in corrupt or ridiculous forms. This may be seen as expressive of our collective decadence, or as a potential seeding of the consciousness of the future. Obviously dedicated magicians believe the second to be true, with the crucial proviso that the art must be refined and purified repeatedly. Paradoxically this purification brings us to very simple early forms of magic related to the growth of consciousness and the relationship between the worlds.

If this growth and relationship leads to a creative and unified vision of life, magical arts are well justified. The furtherance of this vision is the task of many spiritual traditions and humanitarian organisations; but the transformations which truly enable it are utterly individual. Unless we take responsibility for individual maturity and understanding, the practice of magical arts is valueless. In esoteric terms, the acceleration of magical energies at the present time is often seen as the direct result of dedicated practice and development by modern workers; this is a more responsible attitude than the old-fashioned notion that 'hidden masters' are going to appear and suddenly put the world right. Nor does this taking of justified responsibility in any way conflict with the overview of divinity or spirit enlivening human hearts and souls if only they choose to respond.

The future of magical arts is now in the hands of actual practising magicians; such persons will create fresh imaginative traditions and methods of transforming consciousness and energy. Some of these methods will be refinements of our inheritance from the collective

190

past; others may be totally new presentations or higher harmonic forms of magic previously unknown.

Our current acceleration towards a possible apocalypse in the form of nuclear war or disaster, and the corresponding need for a spiritual revolution and revelation, are the major concerns of responsible magicians or workers of any spiritually conscious tradition.

APPENDIX I: EXERCISE – INNERWORLD CONTACT

There are several different ways in which innerworld contacts become known to the magician; the most familiar is through the technique of visualisation. There are, however, two further significant manifestations of contact; dreams and direct communication. A number of less common variants on the three modes outlined could be added, but they are either outdated or advanced techniques which are not directly relevant to our present examination and example.

Before proceeding with the exercise, which is based upon visualisation, we should briefly consider both dreams and direct communication. What follows is the shortest possible summary of each, for visualisation, dream contact and direct communication could each take up a book in their own right.

DREAMS

Work with dreams has been dealt with at great length in many books on psychology and in the general stream of esoteric teaching from most ancient times to the present day. Some of the methods relating to dreams are absurdly trivial, while others are based upon techniques of communication and interpretation that have persisted for centuries in various forms. In magical art, dreams are considered selectively rather than inclusively; some are considered valuable, while others are discarded. The guiding rules for such selection vary slightly between esoteric traditions, but generally there are three levels of dream which are identified as follows.

1) *Superficial or eliminatory dreams*, in which the rubbish of daily consciousness is replayed in various disguises. Modern psychology

spends most of its dream analysis on this type of material, which is usually disregarded in esoteric or magical psychology. This mode or type of dream consciousness is recognised by both materialist and magical schools of symbolism to lead directly into the second level.

2) *Highlighted dreams* are those in which the interior consciousness produces sequences of symbols which are of importance to the dreamer. They can range from a presentation of problems and their solutions to the true innerworld communication filtered through the psychic construct of the dreamer. Such dreams frequently have a quality or impact that enable us to remember them as important, even if we cannot interpret them readily. Such dreams lead into the third level.

3) *Transpersonal or spiritual dreams* are more rare, and employ very specific highly-energised symbols which are also found in the Mysteries, in specific magical and meditational traditions, or in certain religious experiences. They include innerworld contact, usually of high order, and presentations of energies that transform the psyche of the dreamer.

If we refer to the harmonic levels of innerworld contact shown in Figure 19 there is an approximate correspondence between the three levels of dream (which are only working definitions and not firmly separated regions) and the three levels of entity and energy.

1) Eliminatory dreams: elemental contact.
2) Highlighted dreams: ex-human, human and angelic contact.
3) Spiritual dreams: transhuman and archangelic contact.

This correspondence does not, it must be emphasised, suggest that all highlighted dreams are the result of angelic contact or that any such crude direct conclusions may be applied as rules in interpretation. The inference is that harmonics of dream experience in the human psyche are reflections of harmonics of consciousness in the innerworld and the metaphysical worlds, in greater psychic holisms.

There is an enduring method of dream communication employed in magical tuition, which can be dated back at least as far as the Mysteries of classical Greece; it is still successfully applied today. Variations of the technique have been borrowed by modern psychological systems, but in our present context the emphasis is not upon therapy but upon innerworld contact. Magic regards self-realisation and integration as a natural side-effect of spiritual growth, and not as a therapy or end in itself.

A magical dream arises out of *ritual intention*, out of the conscious waking use of symbols and patterns that will attune the consciousness of the individual during sleep.

The Magical Dream

Before sleeping, the magician defines and opens the Circle, attunes to the principle patterns, and meditates briefly. This method is directed towards a request for tuition on a specified subject, rather than vague intimations or general 'guidance'. The chosen subject is visualised very clearly, and also may be symbolised by an actual object or image placed upon an altar. Traditionally images such as Tarot trumps have been used for this type of work, due to their convenient size and universal symbolic alphabet. The magician makes a simple avowal to seek further learning on the subject defined during sleep. This method has been used most successfully for direct magical training, and once developed is more reliable and effective than studying from books.

If a known innerworld contact is required, the magician defines this contact through name or image or key symbols. Otherwise the avowal works in a manner similar to a general input to an information network, so the informant or teacher may not be known to the student, and may not even make any sense of presence felt.

In some schools of magic, this method is known as tapping into the 'universal mind', a concept similar that of popular psychology in which the 'unconscious' is said to have answers to all questions. Although the result may be superficially similar, there is a great deal of difference between education through innerworld contact, and unconsciousness providing processes of deduction that are not part of regular mentation. The universal mind is, or should be, defined as a quite different level of perception; stellar, transhuman and archangelic, in which the knower and the known subject merge together. This mode of awareness is one of the highest potentials that we have, and transcends magical work, though it may filter through magical images and methods as our consciousness returns to its exterior direction and habitual rate.

Once the dream-contact method has been established, as described above, the magician pauses each morning on awakening, and writes out whatever can be remembered of dreams on the required subject. If no dreams can be remembered, the subject is written about in any case, and a surprising amount of new material can emerge even if no dream can be consciously recalled. Experienced magicians often rise very early to write out the result of their sleep contact.

DIRECT COMMUNICATION

This method is more obscure, less readily analysed and explained, even in the terms of a magical worldview or vocabulary. As a rule it is not encouraged in early training, as the student may slip into regressive states which result in 'spiritualism' or 'past lives', both of which areas of consciousness are regarded as devolutionary in magical art. The memory of past lives comes into valid use with certain higher modes of consciousness, when the student gains a spiritual overview of personality and incarnation. So-called spiritualism is regarded as a system of interplay with trivial phantoms, or at worst with unhealthy non-human or ex-human entities.

The essence of direct communication lies in attuning the general field of consciousness to the subject in hand (as is done in reading, writing, or normal concentration) while keeping the higher faculties, developed by the five fundamental arts and disciplines of magic, open and receptive. With practice this results in an active dialogue between the magician and his or her innerworld contacts. It does not, therefore, involve trance, hypnosis, or even a very deep level of meditational withdrawal or visualisation, though images will often arise in the inner vision as a result of a correct balance and dialogue.

There is little similarity between this method and those of commercial mediumship or clairvoyance, for, rather than being a blank page, the magician employs his or her levels of consciousness as polarised exchanges or layers of interface between the innerworld contact and the human contact. The vexed question of the location of the communicators is actually irrelevant; the contact arises from somewhere else and filters through the carefully attuned and balanced receptive/active psyche. In some cases the contact seems to be behind the magician, speaking as it were over his shoulder; this is often a feature of communicative dreams.

Direct communication is a variant of *Mediation*, but applied in a more casual circumstance than highly-charged ritual, and fused into verbal or imaginal units rather than in direct magical power flowing through the mediator.

ESTABLISHING AN INNERWORLD CONTACT

The following exercise in visualisation is short; it may be undertaken regularly with increasing effect. No specific contact is named in our example, and the method may be used to clarify a number of contacts; with practice it leads to very deep and powerful levels of exchange and communication. Magical art is primarily educational,

195

in the true sense of the word, leading consciousness out of its habitual grooves and fixations. Contacts developed through the imagination are invaluable in our general progress into magical methods, regardless of any debate over the reality of the entities contacted.

1) Open the Circle using either the simple formula given in our exercise *'Opening the Circle'* or any other proven method. It may be helpful to reinforce the Quarters with visualisation, invocation or chant, but lengthy raising of energies is not essential for this type of visualisation.

2) Sitting in the centre of the Circle, which is either a room, dedicated space, or your own body upon the chair, enter into visualisation. This is done by closing your eyes and imagining the pictures described, building them slowly and steadily. In guided visualisation, a script is read, recited or played back upon a tape recorder from a pre-recorded source.

3) *The Visualisation.*
'Before you is a door; it is a plain wooden door set in a high stone wall. You look at this door in the wall for some time until it is utterly clear and solid; as you look you know that the instruction which you seek lies somewhere beyond the entrance that is sealed by the wooden door.

'As you look, you realise that the door will not simply open on demand but only for someone with a valid reason for entry. You meditate upon your reason, clearly defining it in your awareness. In doing so, you inwardly recite a formula for passing through the entrance: "I seek an innerworld contact to teach me the subject of...I seek to pass within under the Light". As you formulate this phrase, you see that a small lamp hangs over the door, with its flame glowing steadily. The door opens, and you rise and pass through the entrance.

'You are in a small courtyard; it is square, surrounded by high stone walls. In the centre is a fountain bubbling from a circular basin. The courtyard floor is of flagstones, inscribed with faint designs. Against each of the four walls there grows a flowering tree, and below the branches of each tree, just to one side of the trunk, there is a door in each wall.

'You walk into the centre of the courtyard, and move from left to right around the fountain, remembering your stated purpose for being admitted. You are waiting for a teacher or adviser to appear through one of the four doors where the blossoms fall. As you pace around the stone basin with its gentle trickle of water, you hear a door open and close quietly behind you. You turn, and place your hands upon the edge of the basin of the fountain. Standing opposite you is your teacher.'

(At this point the effect of the visualisation will vary. Some people cannot see their innerworld contact immediately, and although the door always opens, the contact sometimes remains out of sight, speaking while the magician continues to walk slowly around the fountain. Others may see their teacher immediately. It is very important to remember, and write down at a later time of recollection, the appearance of the contact; his or her face, clothing, any identifying objects or symbols, any suggestions of a name. Sometimes such details take a long time in coming forth; some contacts are reliable for years before the magician sees an image or knows a name. There is no need to try and force a contact to give you a 'name', providing you have a specific mode or symbol of identification.)

There is no further guided part to this visualisation, other than the simple closing pattern which is described in 4 below. For obvious reasons, the subject matter of the interaction between magician and innerworld being will vary infinitely, and only a general summary can be given of what might reasonably occur. After re-stating the subject matter chosen for education or enlightenment (though this is often unnecessary) the magician conducts a conversation with the contact. This is actually a type of mediation combined with images; in advanced stages the imagery fades into a more direct knowledge of the subject in hand.

In the initial stages, the subject matter should be carefully restricted and the time period kept short. Once the magician is attuned to a contact, a series of further inner experiences may be undertaken; the teacher may lead the student through a door, or present specific scenarios through the imagination. The magician, however, should not merely wander about willy-nilly, but keep to the matter in hand. If the contact is within established magical traditions, there will be little or no idle wandering allowed, and a drifting consciousness on the part of the magician will either break the contact or result in a reminder of the function and purpose of the meeting.

If in doubt about time duration, set an arbitrary period of comfortable length, say fifteen or twenty minutes, before starting the visualisation. Our inner clock will usually begin to withdraw the awareness at the time indicated...never use any mechanical means of interruption. The question of duration is subjective, and soon becomes a matter of individual or group style. A summary of the subject matter should be written out as soon as possible after withdrawing from the inner place, though experienced mediators may do so while retaining the inner contact in the imagination.

4) *Closing the Contact.*

'Now the communication is over, you are standing back in the courtyard, with your hands resting upon the bowl of the fountain. A door closes quietly behind you, and you realise that your innerworld contact has departed. You begin to walk slowly from left to right around the square courtyard; suddenly you feel prompted to stop in front of one of the flowering trees; you know intuitively that the door by this tree is the one that leads to your own outer world. There may be a symbol or object hanging from the lower-most branches; if there is, remember it, for it is a key to further experience in the innerworld, a key which may be used to pass to and fro easily. The door opens, and you see your room and chair beyond. You pass through, and hear the door close behind you. Slowly you merge back into the image of yourself seated in a room, facing the stone wall and the closed door. The image of the wall dissolves, and you open your eyes. All that remains is to close the Circle according to your custom.'

5) *Closing the Circle.*

The Circle is closed either by using our example formula *'Closing the Circle'* or through the methods to which you are accustomed. You write out your experience, and if possible write a commentary upon the experience. This last is a very useful method, as much will come of a commentary that is not realised in the initial description or summary of the innerworld teaching and experience.

If required, you can pursue the subject matter further in sleep the same night, using the method outlined for magical dreams, again writing out results in the early morning.

APPENDIX II:
OPENING THE CIRCLE

Although the basic elements of this type of ritual have been included in the preceding chapters, a coherent short presentation such as the following should be learnt by heart. From such a simple foundation the ritualist will eventually build and develop a structure for a lifetime of magical work.

1) Sit and approach Silence inwardly.
2) On emerging from Silence, use the Crossing formula.

IN THE NAME OF THE STAR FATHER,	(above)
THE DEEP MOTHER,	(below)
THE TRUE TAKER,	(right)
AND THE GREAT GIVER,	(left)
ONE BEING OF LIGHT...AMEN.	(encircle)

3) Light a flame, which is passed to a taper for candles. Use the Hexagram formula for the main altar candle or lamp.

BLESSED IS THE LIGHT THAT COMES AMONG US,	(downward Triangle)
BLESSED IS THE LIGHT THAT LIVES WITHIN US,	(upward Triangle)
BLESSED IS OUR BEING ONE IN LIGHT.	(encircle Hexagram)

4) Opening the Quarters:
   a) Light flame at Quarter and make Hexagram sign, saying:
      BLESSED BE THE LIGHT ARISING IN THE (EAST),
      IN THE NAME OF THE SON OF LIGHT...AMEN.
   b) Open Gate at each Quarter by visualisation or signs.
5) Stand in centre of Circle with arms upraised (to the Stars).

IN THE NAME OF THE STAR FATHER,	(lower arms to point downwards)
AND OF THE DEEP MOTHER,	

THE FOUR GATES ARE OPEN AND
THE ELEMENTS AND WORLDS ASSEMBLED...
AMEN.

A long resonant chant of *AMEN* in which the energy in the Circle is visualised being charged with a complementary energy rising up out of the Earth.

6) Conduct invocation: Use the *Invocation of the Son of Light* or another invocation as required for specific work.

CLOSING

This is conducted by circling and closing each Quarter, with a Crossing sign. After all lights are extinguished (the first light to be lit is the last to be extinguished) a brief meditation upon Silence is conducted.

GLOSSARY OF TERMS

ABYSS, THE   The void between our solar system and others; the void between individualised and transcendent consciousness; the void between the Supernal and lower Spheres of the Tree of Life, created by the Fall into manifestation.

ANGELS   Traditional term for aspects of cosmic consciousness typified as 'messengers' or carrying enabling entities.

ARCHANGELS   Traditional term for aspects of universal consciousness, typified as 'proclaimers' or primal enabling entities.

ARCHETYPES   Matrices for the energies of the universe, primal patterns.

CONTACTS   (Innerworld) Beings who relate magical systems from the Innerworlds; includes Teachers, Guardians, Guides, Mediators and many others.

CONTEMPLATION   The wordless, formless, fusion of consciousness with a chosen subject.

ELEMENTALS   Traditional term for aspects of Elemental consciousness typified as entities of one strongly emphasised Element (Air, Fire, Water, or Earth).

ELEMENTS   Four relative states of power in expression.

EX-HUMAN BEINGS   Human consciousness or beings in dimensions or states beyond the regular outer world, but not Trans-human.

GODS and GODDESSES   Conscious images or imaginal forms embodying universal and environmental energies. Used as specific magical images in visualisation, deriving from various coherent traditions and religions (not idols).

GLYPHS   'Maps' or simple geometric patterns used in magic.

HOLISM(S)   A natural unity or 'whole' reflected through many parts.

201

IMPLEMENTS Four symbols of balance: Sword, Rod, Cup, Shield.

INITIATE One who has begun to be transformed through magical arts.

INNERWORLD A dimension or construction of images, energies, and shared consciousness attuned to chosen Archetypes.

KABBALAH (QABALAH) A Jewish mystical tradition often borrowed and misrepresented in Western literature.

MAGICAL IMAGES Specific constructions within the imagination. May relate to images found in religion worldwide, or may be unique to esoteric traditions or systems.

MEDITATION
The discipline of directing consciousness inwardly upon chosen subjects.

METAPHYSICS The science of dimensions, energies and Worlds that transcend and underpin the regular world of manifestion. A higher order of physics.

MYTH A story epitomising true relationships between humans, other life forms, and the universe.

PATHS Connective energies and images upon the Tree of Life.

POWER CENTRES Traditionally represented as centres or locations of energy within the human entity. These centres are consciously awakened and aligned by magical arts.

RITUAL The fusion of creative imagination with expressive action.

SEERSHIP The development of dynamic inner vision and its accurate meaningful expression as words or images.

SIGILS Specific symbols or 'letters' used as visual guides for ritual, meditation, contemplation.

SPHERES Polarised energies of existence (see Tree of Life).

SPINDLE, THE The harmonic perception of Moon, Sun and Stars as a central progression of awareness from Earth to the Universe. This is symbolised as a spindle around which all existence turns.

SYMBOLS The imaginative tools and units of energy employed in magical arts. Focal images for specific energies.

TAROT and TAROT TRUMPS A set of picture symbols derived from oral wisdom traditions and later formalised as cards.

TRADITION A collective stream of symbolic education.

TRANSHUMAN BEINGS Advanced individuals of transcendent consciousness, traditionally said to be metaphysical rather than physical.

TREE OF LIFE A pan-cultural symbol of relationship between

Earth and Heaven known in many traditional forms.

VISUALISATION   The art of controlled image making and development of inner vision.

WHEEL OF LIFE   The cycle of the Seasons, Lifetime, Qualities, and Elements in Nature.

WORDS OF POWER   Sonic symbols (see Symbols) which reflect universal qualities of consciousness or energy.

WORLDS   States or harmonics of existence, consciousness, and energy.

BIBLIOGRAPHY

As magical arts are essentially practical, and involve the use of the imagination in directed patterns, this Bibliography is confined to a small number of books for study and supportive material.

Recordings of visualisations, music for magical ritual and meditation, by R.J. Stewart and other specialist authors are available on cassette from Sulis Music, BCM 3721, LONDON WC1N 3XX.

1. *Magical Ritual Methods*, W.G. Gray, Helios Bookservice, Toddington, 1969.
2. *What We May Be*, P. Ferrucci, Turnstone Press, Wellingborough, 1982.
3. *The Mystic Life of Merlin* and *The Prophetic Vision of Merlin*, R.J. Stewart, Routledge and Kegan Paul, London, 1986.
4. *Where is Saint George?* R.J. Stewart, Moonraker Press, Bradford on Avon, 1977 (published by Humanities Press, New Jersey, in the USA).
5. *The Western Way*, Volume One, J. and C. Matthews, Routledge and Kegan Paul, London, 1985 (The Native Tradition).
6. *Mabon and the Mysteries of Britain*, C. Matthews, Routledge and Kegan Paul, London, 1987. *The Mabinogion*, translated G. Gantz, Penguin, Harmondsworth, 1976.
7. *Meditation and Kabbalah*, A. Kaplan, Samuel Weiser, Maine, USA, 1982. *Kabbalah: Tradition of Hidden Knowledge*, Z. Halevi, Thames and Hudson, London, 1979.
8. *The White Goddess*, R. Graves, Faber, London, 1961.
9. *The UnderWorld Initiation*, R.J. Stewart, Aquarian Press, Wellingborough, 1985.
10. *The Western Way*, Volume Two (see 5 above; The Hermetic Tradition).

11. *The Mystic Spiral*, J. Purce, Thames and Hudson, London, 1974.
12. *The Occult Significance of the Blood*, R. Steiner, London, 1907. *Initiation and its Results*, R. Steiner, London, 1910.
13. *The Fire From Within*, C. Castaneda, Black Swan Books, London, 1985.
14. *The Waters of The Gap*, R.J. Stewart, Bath City Publications, Bath, 1981.
15. *Music and the Elemental Psyche*, R.J. Stewart, Aquarian Press, Wellingborough, 1987.
16. *The Key to the Tarot*, A.E. Waite (handbook for the Waite Tarot cards), Rider & Co., London, 1973.
17. *The Treasure House of Images*, G. Knight, Aquarian Press, Wellingborough, 1986.
18. *The Book of Merlin*, R.J. Stewart (editor), Blandford Press, 1987.

The Merlin Tarot, a full colour deck of Tarot cards, by R.J. Stewart and Miranda Gray, will be published in 1988. A book describing the Merlin Tarot system in detail will accompany the deck.

AFTERWORD AND INVITATION

The emphasis of this book has been on personal direct effort and experience; you cannot be a magician unless you honestly and repeatedly work at the art. I am aware that much of the material offered is different from regular 'occultism', but can only remind the reader that what generally passes for magical art in literature is mainly literary or journalistic fabrication by authors who have little or even no practical experience of the subject. Alternatively, the small minority of true magicians have frequently shrouded their tuition in secrecy and obscurity, either as a result of living in a cruel suppressive culture or as part of the subtlety of tuition through paradox and riddling humour.

As an author I receive frequent letters from people who want to join a magical group or order; the only true answer to this type of enquiry is that if you work seriously and directly with the magical arts you will eventually come into contact with like-minded people or magical orders. Joining social groups, classes or mail-order courses is one of the worst possible ways of discovering the truth about magical arts; it may have a certain negative value as a stage to be grown out of in life, but does very little for the student in terms of true magic. If only such classes taught technique derived from experience, and made no claims towards 'improving life', they might be of considerable value to us all; but this is rarely the case. Conversely, there has been a growing tendency towards group experiential courses held as actual participating events with a non-literary and non-educational or non-intellectual bias; these may form the basis for a revival of an oral tradition of magical tuition, something which is seriously lacking in our culture. But even such gatherings will not replace personal meditation, visualisation and ritual pattern-making.

If you seriously take the material offered in this book and work with it, you will undoubtedly have results from your efforts. While I cannot advise or consult on personal living problems, or offer guidance or membership of magical orders, I would be very pleased to hear from any reader or group who wishes to write to me, care of the publisher. If you enclose a stamped addressed envelope, I will do my best to reply to your report, enquiry, or to discuss any genuine subject connected to the magical arts.

R. J. STEWART

INDEX